BRITTANY STONE STORIES

Wendy Mewes

Brittany - Stone Stories

published by Red Dog Books

ISBN: 978-0-9935815-8-8

© Wendy Mewes 2023

The right of Wendy Mewes to be identified as the author of this work is asserted in accordance with sections 77 and 78 of the Copyright Designs and Patents Act 1988

British Library Cataloguing-in-Publication Data
A catalogue record for this book is available
from the British Library

All rights reserved. The publisher's prior written consent is required for any reproduction of this work, in part or in whole, in any form whatsoever.

Illustrations © Alan Montgomery 2023

Red Dog Books is based in Somerset and in Brittany.
Enquiries should be addressed to the editorial office at
Red Dog Books, 29690 Berrien, France.

email: reddogbooks@orange.fr

www.reddogbooks.com

For Lucy Kempton
with love, and thanks for all the seitan

FOREWORD

by Jack Fraser

"Stones tell stories and we tell stories about stones."

The first time I visited Brittany I wanted to look at rocks. Not just any rocks – my visit was generally centred round the admiration of megaliths. Standing stones, burial chambers, stone circles – these are the things I like to look at, and my love of lichen and the comfort I get from moorland scenery is connected to this. There are lots of prehistoric sites in Brittany, but I was astonished to find on my first visit that there were so many sites close to where I was staying that I didn't even make it to Carnac, very much the most famous but not, perhaps, the most atmospheric or inspiring of the sites in Morbihan.

I've often lamented the fact that without a real grasp of either French or Breton it's hard to pick up anything but very basic information about Brittany's prehistoric monuments – sites often have interpretation boards, but they're usually tri-lingual (a good thing, but it does mean there's not much space for folklore). This book goes a long way to balancing that out, as it's full of the sort of stories I'd be well aware of if these were British sites, but which in this case were all new to me. I love learning new things and every page deepened my understanding of this wonderfully fascinating place.

Although my main interests are archaeological, learning more about the place of the stones in the landscape and the impact that has had on the people who lived near them over the last two thousand and more years is always appealing. The tensions between the Church and what was going on before Christianity came to Brittany, and the similar, earlier tensions between the Romans and the Iron Age communities make for colourful stories, and the way these are interpreted later, as interest in 'the Celts' grew and waned over the 19th and 20th centuries, all contribute to a rich and fertile ground for the imagination.

Churches, calvaries and *fontaines* are as unavoidable in Brittany as the megaliths. Holy springs have their own folklore, and although it may be hard to get any idea of what people believed before the saints settled on their watery gifts, it's always good to know exactly which bits of yourself you should be dipping in the water. I certainly wasn't aware of how many of Brittany's saints were evangelising Welsh and Englishmen.

I've never visited a Chaos – described in Chapter one – but could there be a better name for anything. It perfectly encapsulates the almost terrifying sense of movement found in a valley stuffed with rocks. So huge as to be eternal and yet so clearly brought there by the unimaginably immense powers of nature. In Britain the Victorians loved this sort of thing and clearly the artists and writers of France were equally drawn to such places, leading the way for later tourists. We're used to this sort of grandeur on the coast but finding it damply concealed within a forest is something else entirely. You can't help wondering if seeing these places helped inspire the people who first raised a menhir, all those rocks, lying temptingly exposed just asking you to pick out the best ones to raise as megaliths or use to construct a burial chamber.

My obsession with standing stones has led to several trips to Brittany without once visiting a château, which seems quite shocking really. I've rectified this now but for some reason, despite a childhood spent visiting the ruined castles of England and Wales, it never occurred to me that I might see such things in France. The descriptions in this book of Château de Guildo and Fortresse de Largoët are full of tempting detail and I'll be adding them to my list for the next trip. I particularly love a 'wild' castle – a romantically picturesque ruin without ticket sales. Although I like to learn about things, I do also like a bit of mystery, and always enjoy the sensation that I'm experiencing a site as famous visitors of the past may have done.

Although I've seen for myself a number of the places described, perhaps the one that felt most significant to me is the Venus of Quinipily, which I discovered by accident in 2022. The leaflet you get when you visit is only able to provide a limited amount of information, but the Venus's story is one of the most extraordinary of all those in this book, and her complex and embattled history a strong contrast to the place she now finds herself. She probably raises more questions than can ever be answered, and who knows what further stories she'll gather to herself in the future.

Even if you've been visiting or living in Brittany for twenty years, I think you'll find plenty in this book to interest you and help you find intriguing places to visit.

CONTENTS

	page
Introduction	1
1. Chaos	15
2. Stony Words	35
3. Cover	46
4. Elevation	68
5. Stone Boats	90
6. Surround	96
7. Celebrity	118
8. Remnant	133
9. Transformation	157
10. Performance	178
11. Memorial	194
12. Ex-stones	213
Acknowledgements	220
Further reading	221
Index	222

ILLUSTRATIONS by Alan Montgomery

	page
Les Causeurs, Île de Sein	7
Chapelle de Saint Samson, Pleumeur-Bodou	9
Chaos de Mardoul	16
Pink Granite Coast, the Bottle	22
Gorges du Corong	30
Petit Menec	36
Chapelle Saint Hervé, Mené Bré	43
Arthur's Grotto, Huelgoat	51
Ti-ar-Boudiged, Brennilis	58
Hermitage of Saint Hervé	64
Menhir de Kerloas	70
Église Lampaul-Guimiliau	78
Calvaire, Trégastel	83
Saint Conogan's stone boat	92
Fontaine de Barenton	102
Chapelle de Prad Paol	106
Venus de Quinipily	114

	page
Menhir du Champ Dolent	*125*
Roche aux Fées	*128*
Château de Saint-Aubin-du-Cormier	*133*
Château du Guildo	*136*
Donjon, Fortresse de Largoët	*145*
Manoir de Coecilian	*152*
Babouin, menhir	*159*
Sainte-Tréphine, stele	*162*
Menhir de Saint Uzec	*165*
Coët Correc, allée couverte	*168*
Pierres sonnantes	*179*
La Roche tremblante	*182*
Ankou, Lannédern	*195*
Monument aux marins 1914-1918, Pointe Saint-Mathieu	*209*
Allée couverte du Rocher (from an old postcard)	*214*
Alignement de la Madeleine	*216*

Born in Scotland, **Alan Montgomery** is a historian, writer and guide who now splits his time between London and Morbihan.

INTRODUCTION

Rumengol. Famous shrine to the Virgin Mary. A focus of pilgrimage for centuries. And what is depicted in the stained-glass window above the main altar - the Crucifixion? The Annunciation? No, it's a dolmen. A neolithic burial place. Welcome to Brittany.

This tiny village just poking out of the glorious Forêt du Cranou has long been a *haut lieu* of Christianity in Finistère. It is also the setting of a curious legend and entwined traditions, brimming with Druids and old stones, saints and blood sacrifice. Of which that window remains the only legacy on the ground, relating the foundation story of the magnificent church dominating a little knoll, and extended by an open air chapel to cope with the crowds flowing in for the blessing of Notre-Dame de Rumengol.

Stones tell stories and we tell stories about stones. Brittany is well-known as a land of mystery and otherness, and stones lie at the heart of its identity. Stone is about survival through transformation, a whole language of landscape, telling us of the past and inspiring our own interpretation through narrative. Stones can be like people in history, with a symbolic role in their own locality. This region is perhaps at the origins of megalithic creation in Europe, and certainly heavily founded on later Celtic myths and Christian traditions, distinguishing narrowly between life here and life beyond the screen of death, between days gone by and the present moment. So much of this is expressed through the permanence of stone in one form or another, from remnants of ancient mountains to the omnipresent monuments. Many natural sites are significant sources of folklore, but the megaliths in particular, human constructs as they are, often speak loudest of the distant past's allure, unknown and unknowable.

The stained glass window at Rumengol was created in 1886 by Léopold Lobin de Tours, presenting the origin legend of the site in place of the earlier more conventional representations of the annunciation and nativity. The end of the 19th century in Brittany was both a time of enormous Celtic and folklore revival and a great increase in the size of Christian congregations, leading to the elaboration of churches. Both represent a fervour of searching for faith and identity in the generation before the shattering impact of WWI. For Notre-Dame de Rumengol, the original church of 1536 was a victim of its own success which resulted in not only an extension of the nave, but the addition of that large outdoor chapel to accommodate the huge numbers attending the annual Pardons.

So what's it all about? Here's the story, which even manages to cut in the Breton Atlantis legend, the drowning of the city of Ys (see p.97). This cataclysmic event took place in the Bay of Douarnenez, and saw King Gradlon of Quimper escape from the waves by dint of jettisoning his wayward daughter Dahut from the back of his horse, on the advice of spiritual counsellor, Saint Guénolé. Afterwards the two men were roaming on the summit of Menez Hom overlooking the bay, when they turned inland and saw smoke rising from a distant fire. Which of the two is the instigator in what follows varies according to the teller, but all can agree on the outrage of discovering that the fire related to Druidic ritual of human sacrifice on a special stone in the deep forest of Cranou. Either the king immediately vowed to destroy this pagan sanctuary and build a church on the very spot of desecration or the saint insisted on rushing to the scene at once to put a stop to such profanity, which ill befitted Gradlon's newly Christian kingdom. But they were of one mind. Off they went.

Quite how they succeeded in calling time on these heathen proceedings is not related, but the scene on the window gives up the telling aftermath. It incorporates various layers of composition and significance. Most striking is the dolmen, under a spreading oak tree, a large slab raised like a table on two smaller ones, just right for a bit of blood-letting. But now it has been sanitised to the extent that rather than a mutilated body, we find the Virgin Mary and Holy Child sitting in anachronistic glory on top of the stone. Her presence is powerfully symbolic to Christians, sweetly soothing away those thorny pagan issues of violence and fertility. Below, women pray, one clutching her child (maybe saved from sacrifice?), and a repentant Druid in red cloak prostrates himself on the ground. Villagers congregate under the trees watching the scene. In the centre, King Gradlon offers a model of the church he has promised, the church which, in most recent format, the window depicting this scene now adorns. Saints Corentin and Guénolé keep the profane at bay. And then in the bottom corner, a sad figure clad in yellow. A defeated bard hides his head in his robe and cries, holding his harp, now broken and useless. The message is simplistically clear: the triumph of Christianity over an older, barbaric religion. The Church is master now. It was evidently not as simple as that.

This tale may be relatively late, inspired by one man's interpretation of the name Rumengol itself. We'll look at stony vocabulary in more detail later on, but here only the basic Breton word for stone - '*men*' - is needed. The Chevalier de Freminville, a naval officer, prolific antiquarian and avid cross-dresser, writing in 1835, claimed that the word signified a red, glowing stone from *ruz-men-goulou* (red, stone, light(s)) and that this was in fact a stone which once stood where the church is now, a focus for pagan rites. He describes the trees of the forest as 'century old oaks which shaded the mysterious ceremonies of the Druids'. The stone itself inevitably attracted the hostility of early Christians in the area, just as they themselves attracted the hostility of certain pagan inhabitants. The lord of nearby Le Faou was to slaughter a couple

3

of saints in the church at Daoulas a little later to show his contempt for the incomers and their new religion. Other investigators of the origin of the shrine's name preferred a more prosaic meaning for Rumengol: *Remed-oll*, the complete remedies (of the Virgin), which is recorded in the archives, and is naturally the version more acceptable to the church. A contemporary of the Chevalier, Emile Souvestre, in his *Le Finistère in 1836* prefers this interpretation, speaking of Notre-Dame-de-Tous-les-Remèdes.

Interestingly, Freminville regarded the unusual number of four Christian Pardons later celebrated at Rumengol, instead of one annual saint's day celebration, as derived from earlier rites around the solstices and equinoxes in Celtic tradition, and this does seem a site where ancient religion has not been entirely forgotten. Even the canticle of Notre-Dame de Rumengol sung in Breton in the most devout of religious processions contains an allusion to the Roman poet Lucan's chilling invocation of worship of savage Teutatès. This reference to the Druids' merciless blood sacrifices in the dark woods, suggests that the foundation legend is well-established in local tradition.

> Var ar mean-ruz e skuillet goad
> Hag er C'hrannou e kreiz ar c'hoat,
> A zindan derven Teutatès,
> Tud veze lazet eb True.

> On the red stone, blood was spread
> And in the middle of the wood at Cranou
> Under the oak of Teutatès
> People were killed without pity.

The Pardon of the Trinity is probably derived from summer solstice celebrations, and it was said in local folklore that on Trinity

Sunday, King Gradlon and Saint Guénolé continued to appear on Menez Hom, visible from the church precinct, to check that the faithful at Rumengol were keeping to Christian tradition and had not lapsed into pagan ritual. In 1859 Edouard Valtin said that four times a year 12-15,000 pilgrims arrived at Rumengol for cures at the sacred *fontaine* blessed by the Virgin Mary. Today there remain two Pardons, in June and for the Assumption in August. No Druid sacrifices scheduled as far as I know.

This inter-relation between early Christianity and paganism provides the richest, most revelatory source of stories involving stones in Brittany. The Edict of Arles, a papal decree of 452, urged the destruction of scared trees, springs and stones revered in pre-Christian society at a time when the new religion was intent on imposition. It was to be followed by other similar pronouncements, but there was also a more pragmatic movement of assimilation, the result of which we see today in sacred places which preserve both elements. Pope Gregory in the early 7th century went from urging eradication to decreeing that pagan temples should be sprinkled with holy water and given altars and relics, encouraging people to make the switch and reuse their former sites of worship with new focus. This more prudent approach, mindful of powerful local attachments, may be of the greatest relevance to many sites in Brittany. So standing-stones were engraved with Christian symbols or topped with crosses, chapels and *fontaines* were built by water sources, sometimes alongside menhirs and Iron Age steles, while the whole circus of saints and their miracles staked claim to the creation of pagan sites or reduced stones to objects of their powers.

Today at Rumengol we have only the story and no stone, but there is no shortage of surviving stones complete with their stories. Even the remote stone circle on the loneliest tip of the island of **Ouessant**, 25 kilometres out into the Atlantic, may well have been the target of an evangelising St Pol (Paul Aurelian) on his arrival from Cornwall, determined to drive out the pagan priestesses who frolicked there without restriction. It is said that he drove the 'wild women' away from the stones, although they just took themselves off to the other end of the isle and waited for the wave of saints – Corentin and Guénolé also turned up – to pass. The isolated site of the circle has become part of his legend, with a nearby cross erected in 1702 and a direct association with other perfectly innocent rocks in the vicinity as Pol's special places of prayer and meditation. The taking back of territory is at play here, on the ground as well as in the hearts and minds of the inhabitants. He may still be the patron of the church, but the neolithic monument also still stands, mysterious and evocative of another layer of history altogether.

This endurance of pre-Christian places, stories and practices, and their mingling almost nonchalantly with those of the Church, is one of the great strengths of the Breton tradition. It is mostly thanks to the power of oral transmission that preserves (and transforms) them down the generations, without relying on books and the ability to read. This culture was very much of the ordinary people, fostered around the hearth, cherished down familial lines. It has ensured that the past is never left behind, and remains vivid in the popular imagination, along with the enduring passion for local heritage that enlivens every corner of Brittany even today. But there is no avoiding the popularly acclaimed Breton saints in the context of special stones in the region, which have become a focus for their miracle-working. These holy men and a few women, arrived on the coast of Armorica (the land of the sea) from Great Britain in the 5th-7th centuries, and were instrumental in the foundation of what was later to become Brittany.

Many neolithic monuments have been damaged and lost, whether from Christian destruction (to make way for a church or chapel), tomb-robbers, agricultural land clearance, simple recycling for construction of houses, walls and roads or just a nice bit of granite or schist to stick in the garden. But there are many wonderful examples of pagan and Christian monuments co-existing, sometimes at decidedly close quarters. The church on the **Île de Sein**, enlarged to meet the needs of a population swollen by fishermen from Paimpol at the end of the 19th century, was built right alongside two magnificent menhirs, known as *Les Causeurs* (*Ar Brigourien* in Breton or the Chatters), as the stones appear to be talking to one another. It is quite possible that these were part of a stone circle or alignment whose other components are now lost. The island's reputation for pagan association had been set in the first century AD by Roman historian Pomponius Mela, who told of nine virgin weather witches, the Senes, who could control the elements, shape-shift and effect cures.

Les Causeurs, Île de Sein

At the **Chapelle de Saint-Samson** in the countryside of Pleumeur-Bodou, a very modest standing-stone was moved into the church precinct during the reformist zeal of the early 17th century. Rather than being destroyed, it was transformed, and now has a curiously splayed tip, like a flower or a dog's paw, although it's supposed to have been deliberately shaped in the form of a cross to remove its earlier phallic air, when young ladies used to rub themselves (naked) against it in the hope of bearing a child. The stone was also said to be effective against backache, and so popular with Breton wrestlers (practitioners of the *gourenn*) who brushed up against it before bouts. Little this menhir may be but modern geomancers give it a high energy rating and it certainly has a strong presence for such a tiny stone, physically dwarfed by the huge solid bell-tower (1610) a few metres away. Two stone monuments, each with their own energy of upward thrust, even if technology had moved on to new heights between the conceptions. The original purpose of the little menhir may have been to mark the spring a short distance away on lower ground, which was made into a sacred *fontaine* with constructed surround in 1632, to claim more 'legitimate' divine power for its healing purposes.

Sometimes the relation between two different forms of ritual was as intimate as it could possibly get with the ancient stones actually incorporated into later buildings. The **Chapelle Saint-Maurice** (an early soldier martyr of Egyptian origin) at Saint Guyomard in Morbihan is a fine example. Although close to a main road, this is an oasis of peace and calm surrounded by little streams and sonorous trees. The spirit of place is very strong. Beside the building, and covered by what looks like a miniature stone house, is a sacred spring, itself a source of miracle cures. Nearby a large lying stone is half in, half out of the east wall of the chapel. The part sticking out into the open, now split into two, was a focus for healing rites, particularly of rheumatism, with pilgrims rubbing the

Chapelle de Saint-Samson, Pleumeur-Bodou

afflicted body part against the stone. An old postcard of the scene carries a text pointing out that the saint had miraculously (it's a long way from any of his stamping grounds) marked the stone with the tip of his sword, just in case anyone got the idea that this was still some pagan nonsense. The connection of stones with healing and fertility rituals continues to the present day, as we shall see.

Megaliths were thought to be products of Celtic civilisation rather than considerably older right up to the 20th century, and particularly associated with lurid Druidic ritual in popular tradition, but also often connected with some of the many types of little people dwelling in the countryside. Research by story collectors of the 19th century broadcast a wealth of tales where fairies built stone 'houses', and the gnome-like tricky *korrigans,* especially prevalent in the Monts d'Arrée, lived under burial chambers and around standing-stones. Such creatures may well distantly derive from the basic Celtic animism that attributed living spirits to all aspects of nature. There is still a real sense here that everything is alive, as anyone spending time in the Breton countryside will discover. The work of the folklorists was vital in recording the repertoire of (mainly elderly) Breton peasants to preserve their personal narratives and popular stories, provide transcripts in Breton and then the translation of the stories into French to benefit a wider audience. This oral tradition is still alive and kicking in Brittany today.

Druidism itself, closely linked to the ancient stones, became a strong part of the great 'Breton movement' of this period with eminent compilers of folklore like Hersart de La Villemarqué (who published the seminal *Barzaz Breiz* in 1839) attending an eisteddfod in Abergavenny the year before, and a generation later, Anatole le Braz (best known for *La Légende de la Mort en Basse-Bretagne*) part of a delegation to Cardiff in 1899. The first assembly of a Breton Gorsedd (bardic convention) took place at Guingamp in 1900, and there is still plenty of contemporary Druidic activity here, notwithstanding various quarrels and schisms in the ranks. Many stone formations are named for this supposedly archaic connection, like the Druids' Cemetery (Pleslin-Trigavou) and the Cordon des Druides, an alignment of more than fifty stones of quartzite at Landéan in Ille-et-Vilaine, as well as sundry 'sacrificial' rocks. These names reflect the popular tradition that Druid ritual was a natural part of country lore.

Overall it was clear that strong local pagan traditions had continued side by side with Christianity through the centuries, often to the despair of church officials. The missionary movement of the 17th century, driven in western Brittany by Michel Le Nobletz and later intensely by his successor Père Julien Maunoir, tried literally to put the fear of God into the ordinary people and bring them back to discipline and focus in their worship. The 'cult of stones' had proved too dear to the peasantry and even many of the clergy of the time, ill-educated and ignorant themselves, who continued the practices of their families without enough recognition of theological issues such as sin and repentance. This period saw much Christianisation of standing-stones, such as that of Saint Uzec (see p. 164) in Pleumeur-Bodou in 1674, a personal initiative of the formidable Père Maunoir.

The nature of stories attached to stones is as various as the stones themselves. They may be primarily for entertainment, or have moral purpose (especially in the hands of the church). Some are generic, some tied to a specific place and borne out of local events. They may be emblematic, adding value to a location, defining the stone(s) as a valued possession of the communal territory. Some are historical or aetiological, others carefully constructed foundation myths or expressions of particular fears, like dangers to travellers. In the absence of knowledge there is always the creative imagination to conjure meaning and significance. Sometimes the narratives are designed to direct and channel views of the past acceptable to the teller, the perpetuation of family glory or national pride. Issues of identity and patriotism can confuse or obfuscate to the extent that sometimes you just can't see the stone for the story.

Tourism has come to learn the value of exceptional stones,

especially megaliths, to the detriment of some sites. Certain monuments have become iconic and for many visitors, size is everything. Carnac is the flag-bearer of the Brittany Megalithic Games, with the inevitable deterioration of physical space and historical atmosphere that millions of feet bring to any location. We'll look at the cult of celebrity in this context. Early postcards, the pioneer form of advertising, preserve many captures of megaliths with posed locals, a clichéd romanticism of the Breton peasant and his family, which attracted considerable numbers of visitors to see these extraordinary relics of a bygone age. The consideration of cultural value really got underway at the end of the 19th century, and this soon transferred into something of significant economic value as industries declined and tourists began to bring more certain money into localities.

But this book is not only about megaliths and their role in the making of sacred landscape, about the Christian chapels that followed and the castles that defended their territories. About humans, in other words. It would be misleading to think that stones only come into their own when manipulated, fashioned or erected by man. Natural rock, apart from intrinsic aesthetic beauty, can spring into life through the results of geological process, chance formation, the interaction with water or unusual intrinsic properties of sound and movement. There's a certain sadness in beautiful granite caves that are deemed not good enough on their own, but suddenly attractive to crowds through forced connection with Merlin or King Arthur. Some places warrant a peep beyond conventional association. Whether nature can only be relevant through human reference is perhaps a question best answered by personal experience. Certainly landscape becomes culturalised through folklore, which adds a top note to the base line of stones, streams and trees. The Chaos de Mardoul described in Chapter 1 is a good example of inspirational stones that have been neither raised up nor brought down by legends. Sometimes to relegate stones without stories to a lesser level is perhaps to miss that deeper connection behind the cultural curtain, a direct synchronicity between 'us and them', a sense of shared space within a natural unity, helping us step back into some purer affiliation.

On a more individual level, what do stones represent for us? The megaliths are the work of our ancestors, so a striving for affinity on a human level is a possibility. Many thought and think that individual stones in neolithic alignments may represent people, notionally or specifically, so perhaps we are looking for our inaccessibly distant past on some subliminal level. We too are of the earth, and stones are like the earliest inhabitants of our land, our forebears. The prodigious folklore of Brittany honours these relics and their continuity of time and space. Natural and erected stones also formed and shaped the physical landscape. They were markers, signposts and boundaries, monuments to the dead. They characterised the world around each local community. Stones were part of childhood and the focus of rituals for ordinary people – finding a partner, fertility rites, healing of a vast multitude of conditions. They were there – enduring and secure, a vital force pinning down the fabric of communal life, even as field boundaries altered and properties changed hands.

There are after all so many ways of looking at stones, and no denying an immensely powerful attraction between humans and characterful examples. It is perfectly possible to form strong bonds with rocks, the same emotional connection that is deemed quite natural with trees which are more obviously living things. Many of the stones highlighted in this book are my friends – although I make no claim that the feeling is reciprocated – in the sense that they are objects of recognition, interest, affection and enquiry, that I derive pleasure from repeated acquaintance and feel better in their company. I know them in a certain sense.

But stones have their own slow life we cannot touch. All of nature was alive in Celtic traditions, and stones are no exception. They are representatives of vast swathes of time, witnesses of history itself. Their existence is long drawn out, but on-going. We may sometimes animate them through our own needs and desires, creating a story or two, drawing attention to them through photographs and videos on social media, but it is the sense of an older, more rooted and hefty existence than our own that draws us in the first place.

The true scale of the difference may be beyond our capacity for understanding. We are moved by the immobility of stones, which we cannot emulate, as well as their ancientness, by the potential stored in their interior. Survival, endurance, experience all inspire awe in our much more limited lives, but that stillness seems to spur some old craving inside us. Yet there is more, because we long to touch them, to feel their depth in our palm, to join our forehead to their fathomless resource, to hold the permanence they represent enfolded in our arms: these few seconds, minutes, hours bring us into the earth and root our own volatile energy.

This book is about Brittany's stones: the stories they tell us and the stories we tell about them.

1 Chaos

Chaos is a good place to start. A time long before man got organised in the world of stone. Part of the vacancy that existed before any creative designer came along, and something rather familiar in the world today: disarray, confusion, a jumble in random form. In Brittany this translates into big heaps of stones. But their origin is far from random, and while various types of rock are susceptible, the characteristic deterioration of granite lends itself to the process. It's a lengthy one, but chaos is a sign of its very nature. The great Hercynian mountains of Europe raised up by tectonic plate action about 350 million years ago would suffer gradual erosion and rising magma chambers which led to the formation of granite from intense heat and intense pressure, then over an infinitesimally slow period of cooling and crystallisation. Surface deterioration began as long as 65 million years ago when rains of a warming climate infiltrated the exposed granite *massifs* and ultimately led to a network of fissures. The rocks eventually split into irregular boulders along these horizontal and vertical *diaclases*, with sitting water producing granitic sand which filled the gaps and finally settled into layers over the surface rocks. It is very much an elemental story of earth, fire, air and water.

When re-exposed, the result was a pile of precarious and increasingly rounded boulders. Gravity eventually took over for those situated on hillside slopes, whilst the sea spitefully shaped the coastal masses. Eventually, the stones tumbled and ended up on the shore or at the bottom of the river valley like a great stash of ill-aimed bowling balls. The narrower the valley, the more dramatic the chaos. Further erosion takes place in situ, at the behest of water. If the heap of rocks is dense and deep enough, this may be invisible, passing beneath, sending its echoing music up through

Chaos de Mardoul

cavernous spaces within the rock pile, or suddenly cascading out in rivulets through gaps. And motion is not necessarily at an end. The notion of falling down is still intrinsic to the chaos, still pertinent. You might almost call it rock and roll.

I have written at length elsewhere about my *nemeton* the **Chaos de Mardoul**, *(Spirit of Place in Finistère),* a deeply numinous yet modest site tucked away in the hilly terrain of Loqueffret. The components are simple, a wide fast-flowing river, littered with granite boulders large and small, the whole starting and stopping abruptly to fill a 200m stretch. The dynamic atmosphere is channelled by the Elez, barrelling down its shallow valley in (frequent) times of serious rainfall. The Chaos is contained between two ancient stone bridges, one exceptionally preserved and four slabs wide, but sometimes submerged as it lies low in the water, with the other only half surviving in uneven form and finished off by recent extension. Because these are impractical for the farm vehicles of today, there are also two modern versions of metal tubes and concrete to top and tail it all.

In winter a veritable torrent drives along this valley and most of the path is flooded. At other times it is possible to cross the flow by jumping from rock to rock, or perch in the middle on a solid base in the heart of the river. Part of its unusual appeal is the absence of specific legends, resulting in a purity of perception that lets nature be what nature is, a rare phenomenon. The rocks intermingle with vegetation characteristic of the *landes* (moors), oak, willow and alder, gorse, broom and ferns, lining the banks. One enormous rock dominates the left bank, overlooking the chaotic scene. It has a shallow depression in the top which immediately conjures claims of a platform for ritual killing. I don't know about human sacrifice, but I once saw people making love on top of this pinnacle, confirming the notion that passionate energy permeates this place.

The Elez has come down from the heights of the Monts d'Arrée where it rises near Saint Rivoal. The chaos appears between the great reservoir by the nuclear power station at Brennilis and a hydro-electricity plant at Saint Herbot, where access is now blocked to the wonderful cascades, once a famous tourist attraction. Here there is local legend of the giant Hok Bras (also connected to nearby Huelgoat), who is said to be buried under a hill, and commemorated with a carving under one of the choir stalls in the lovely chapel in Saint Herbot. This image is appropriate as it ties in with the traditional popular theory of how the chaotic phenomenon came into being in the first place. The narrative now moves to human perspective.

Chaos' essential element of disarray ties the form metaphorically to the pre-civilised world, a time without order or social mores, with a randomness of shape and function that comes from the will of nature not mankind. It is orderless matter before fashioned creation. It is mess and tangle, showing an unpromising lack of restraint or respect for order. It represents in legend the barbaric era of the giants, those brainless connoisseurs of violent vulgarity, but big and ugly enough to heft enormous boulders with ease, the ideal actors on the stage of a primitive landscape. So the foundation myths of chaos in Brittany involve rocks as pesky irritants in an ogre's shoe, missiles thrown in anger between warring groups and the product of colossal indigestion.

Behind such a shambles must be ungovernable behaviour with no thought for consequence. That the rocks might be giants' weapons or their rubbish indicates the sad state of affairs before gods turned up to polish up the world into neater lines. A good chaos looks like what it is, the result of some serious ill-discipline, like paint spattered indiscriminately on canvas, but on a geological time scale. There is no controlling chaos, although church propaganda did later seek to domesticate it, with saints and angels coming to be associated with these rude cathedrals of nature in the period when God (allegedly) brought structured planning through the Christian religion. So challenging is the appearance of chaos that it had to be reclaimed for system and subservience.

The essential nature of chaos is formless, but it is its very form that has attracted interest in modern times. Bizarre stony shape prompts speculation and the exercise of creative muscles, which leads to that popular pastime of imposing the human dimension on something elemental. For the chaos today is primarily an activity of the imagination, a game of pseudo identification. Naming takes away the mysterious threat of uncontrolled unknowns, animating this natural phenomenon by dragging and name-dropping fairies, saints, household utensils and Napoleon's hat into the picture. Other chaotic legends sprang from the notion of hiding place and concealment. Various fugitive Chouans, the staunchly Catholic late 18th century anti-revolutionaries, are said to have sought shelter in the murky spaces of chaos from marauding Republicans, drawn to a fitting setting for tales of light and shadow. A true story is that some of the poorest of the poor, at the beginning of the 20th century, came from necessity to live in tiny handmade troglodyte hovels roughly forced into the rocks of the chaos along the Pink Granite Coast. Somehow this is almost as evocative as the giants.

Chaos is truly a graphic gift for invention and tourist amusement. So we learn at an early stage of our exploration that this singular natural phenomenon requires interpretation and enhancement to rise above the level of a pile of rocks. Just stoniness is not enough. Just awesomeness, in the literal sense of the word, is not enough. Chaos has to work for its living and entertain us, although this turns out to be true of so many of the other stones in Brittany. Once such layers are piled on, you have something in a different dimension, and rocks are more object than subject. But there is no doubt that tales are what visitors like and expect.

The chaotic throng of the **Côte de Granit Rose (Pink Granite Coast)**, associated mainly with the town of Perros-Guirec, glows under summer sunshine. It really is the vivid colour of its name thanks to the preponderance of alkaline feldspath crystals, rich in impurities of hematite (iron oxide) in the composition of the rock, together with black mica and a shiny greyish white quartz. The nuance of pink depends on the degree of oxidisation. The hue is certainly warming and showy, and the shapes sensational in any light. This is not, however, really a place of legend. Fantasy is the theme: it's a bit like a drive-by art exhibition, with masterpiece after masterpiece of visual entertainment laid out before one's eyes. Using what was originally the coastguards' path, where officers patrolled for the chance of capturing smugglers, the viewing route weaves along past a display of supreme exhibitionism. But this chaos is regulated and manicured with levelled surfacing and noticeboards, and interspersed with more modern structures. There's the lifeboat station, a look-out post from the 18th century, a powder-store, the iconic little lighthouse, a former pre-war garage now festooned with gargoyles like a pagan temple, and the unusual oratory of Saint Guirec situated on the rocky beach at Ploumanac'h, where the firework display of outlandish formations temporarily comes to an end.

This chaos is all about light, a truism for coastal walking in general, but here the rock merits the trouble of choosing early morning or sunset for the most spectacular effects. The contrast between veins of quartz, gleaming granite and dark gneiss on the beaches is somehow primeval in itself, especially where younger granite has forced its way into the 2-billion-year-old stygian layer. And long before its aesthetic aspects were valued for their own sakes, these stones played a practical part in spreading the word of Brittany's lithic riches. Coastal quarrying was once intense here with the jazzy rocks much in demand and sea transport to many far-flung destinations right at hand. Prolific exploitation of the pink stuff at La Clarté beside the mysterious Vallée des Traouïero (Valley of the valleys), with its granite grottoes and wild vegetation, lasted up until the early 20th century, but now only one or two remain. To be seen a little distance to the east of all this glamour, the actual *granite de Perros*, for which Perros is not famous, is beige-coloured, but no-one talks about that.

Remembering that this vast chaos was once a vertical mountain maybe 6000m tall many million years ago, and finally brought low by the actions of the same sea that toys with it now, perhaps helps to envisage this striking edge in the context of time. Following the trail from the Plage de Trestraou in Perros gives a build-up of anticipation as it takes a kilometre or so for the first big formation in a transformed palette to come into view, but once in amongst it, the wonders come thick and fast. The Château is a rocky mass of fissures beautifully illustrating the origins of chaos whilst maintaining its structure for the moment. A chaos in waiting. The name is an obvious one, as its protruding perch on the edge looks chosen for defence, and the rock has the rough lines of a square-cut castle of impressive bulk. Next up is the Devil's rock, a hanging outcrop which just about offers the profile of a witch if viewed from the right angle with a bit of mental effort.

The names of oddly shaped rocks are well-known, but some of these identifications are harder work than others. No-one has any problem with the Bottle (*renversée* or knocked over), a hanging rock balanced precariously on a large block. The nearby Chameleon is fittingly less obvious and something of a strain to pick out. Maybe wait as it changes colour in the light. The Sea Tortoise could be a UFO and the Tables of the Law really do very little to live up to that grandiose description. But that's the point. Extravagance and individualisation are necessary to enhance this breath-taking natural site. The mass can seem overwhelming, and it can make your eyes ache, raking back and forwards over literally thousands of bright stones in strong sun. My personal favourite is the Baked Bean: good luck with finding it. Such harmless fun is the level at which these

Pink Granite Coast, the Bottle

rocks work (given that sheer beauty isn't often rated top of the criteria list these days). There are no stories in these coastal rocks themselves, just an amusing game, exploring the quirky spirit of the human imagination. Doing this brings them into our remit, makes them our toys rather than the giants' playground they resemble. It brings them down to a more manageable scale. The geological fascination is less obviously appealing.

On the rocky route out to the lighthouse, a bizarre lick of rock does indeed resemble the wave of its nickname, one destined never to break except maybe under the weight of tourists climbing onto it for photos. The events attached to this area are more prosaic. The original light-house, built in 1860, was actually in grey granite from Île Grande, and a few blocks from this construction can be seen on the sand below the current building. Destroyed during WWII, it was resurrected in pink granite in 1947, and took its new name for the new colour: Phare Men Ruz - remember what that means? It is now the main image used in tourist publications for this iconic stretch of coastline, although from the foot of the tower, the lantern looks distinctly like a mini Michelin man in red hat and trousers. As the sun sets on the Pink Granite coast, intensifying the shades of *granit rose,* I can't help thinking the Chevalier de Freminville would have enjoyed the spectacle of this glowing 'red rock' and maybe envisaged Druid sacrifice on a vast scale.

Soon after the Death's Head rock, one of the most gratifying likenesses, the route turns inland and comes out again at the Plage de Saint Guirec. An oratory to this holy man stands on the beach, surrounded by water as the tide comes in. The old wooden statue where young women stuck pins in the saintly nose to ensure marriage within a year, has been replaced by a stone image, and some ugly recent renovation. On the hill above the beach, a last wonder stands in a private garden. The rock is known as Napoleon's Hat, for obvious reasons, but it does at least have greater historical resonance than, for example, the Rabbit (hint: turn your head sideways). On 3rd August, 1944, the BBC broadcast a message to signal general uprising against the German occupying forces to the Breton resistance: *Le chapeau de Napoléon est-il toujours à Perros?* 'Is Napoleon's hat still at Perros?'

The great man has another connection with the pink stone. Having admired the ancient Egyptian monuments at close hand, he wanted to construct a great memorial to his armies in the rosy granite of the Côtes Nord. (This was the name of the department of Brittany now known as Côtes d'Armor up until 1990, when something chilly in that appellation, which certainly didn't stand well with the lovely warm glow of the famous granite, urged change.) Napoleon went as far as instructing a director of the project and sent an architect to discuss extraction of suitable stone from La Clarté, but that was before the great Russian debacle, and then the moment had passed.

The key words for the Pink Granite Coast are colour, configuration and convenience. The organised trail is accessible and parking not too distant from the *Maison du littoral* information centre which explains the site to visitors. The combination of hue and light makes a photographer's dreamscape, and who doesn't want to be immortalised next to the Lovers' Rock or a boulder bearing uncanny likeness to a Breton spaniel? It is the refulgent stone that unifies the site, with the sea as an intensifying backdrop to the pieces themselves. The Sept Îles, by contrast, loom in the further distance like pale phantoms. Despite the boats of visitors plying the waves to get a look at their bird colonies, it's hard not to see this little group of islands in their quiet splendour as anything other than a romantically peaceful paradise away from the crowds.

So we might say the Pink Granite coast is the cabaret act of chaos: ostentatious and extremely entertaining. It can leave you feeling well and truly stoned by the end. The north coast of Finistère gives the same exciting configurations in a nice tasteful range of greys. Their setting is also gloriously underpopulated, and I like them better for both reasons. Perros-Guirec to Ploumanac'h is an unashamed tourist mecca. Nothing wrong with that in a way, but it is ultimately so walked and so named, that a sense of discovery or ancientness is elusive. There is no mystery here. Serious action to restrict human access to the authorised trails has enabled the vegetation of the *landes* to regroup and begin to cover this coastal plain again, which is a positive step towards a more natural environment. But there is always going to be a certain irony in such managed and directed chaos…

Huelgoat has the ultimate ingredients for magic: a mature broad-leafed forest spread over steep hillsides interspersed with river valleys, streams and cascades, and most of all ubiquitous evocative granite boulders, some of gargantuan size and many the shape of illusion. The origin stories are predictably gigantesque. Gargantua, the ever popular Rabelaisian figure who features often in Breton folklore, or possibly that more local giant chap, Hok Bras, took offence at the thin gruel offered to him by the inhabitants.

Further north in richer Léon he was given creamy porridge which only emphasised the insult, so he ripped up all the great stones from there and hurled them back at poor old impoverished Huelgoat, leaving a great pile in the Argent valley. It also left more fertile, workable soil in Léon, still today the vegetable capital of Brittany. This tale enshrines an important and real distinction between the two areas in later history. The traditional historical contrast between the poverty of the Monts d'Arrée and prosperity of Léon is a clear factor here, reflecting a long-running cultural saga played out sometimes cruelly, sometimes with grim humour. 'Crows fly on their backs to avoid the miserable sight...' is a well-known saying. Another tamer story pictures the battle between giant inhabitants of Berrien to the north and Plouyé to the south. Most of the boulders they hurled at each other fell short and settled between them in Huelgoat forest.

The main Chaos is right by the centre of the village, accessed by a narrow slippery path through crooked tunnels of rock that would dwarf many of the houses nearby. First stop is the Devil's Grotto where a metal ladder allows descent under the rocks to get splashed by the torrent of water crashing through on its fall from the lake, created in the late 16th century by German engineers to supply the mines in the forest at Locmaria-Berrien. One of those Chouan stories evokes a single rebel in hiding down here toasting a sausage over a fire on a big fork and wearing a big hat, hence throwing an enormous shadow that his pursuers took for the Devil and left well alone... It has also been claimed as a hiding-place for the spoils of female robber Marion de Faouët, who was finally hung in Quimper in 1755 after leading the authorities a merry dance for years.

Passing the open-air theatre to arrive at the top of the valley, chaos lies ahead and continues for quite a distance, filling the hollow with rocks and cavities in equal measure. Those empty spaces are also a crucial ingredient of chaos, kernels of memory from a distant past trapped in the stale air. Underneath flows what will emerge later as the river Argent, so named as its waters were once used at the lead/silver mines. The curved depression is filled with tumbled boulders of all shapes and sizes. In winter the submerged sound of water pounding the furniture in its passage reverberates up from the rocky depths. The valley eventually widens as the river turns, merging with another affluent, and a vast bowl is choked and blocked by giant boulders.

Here you are invited to speculate on the *Ménage de la Vièrge*, the Virgin's Household Utensils, and pick out her bed, cauldron, ladle, etc. It's not an exact art. There's certainly one prominent rock that unmistakably resembles a chicken-leg, but one can no more draw conclusions from that than any of the other traditional associations. As a children's game, it works well (for about two minutes). This domestication of the wild free fall of the chaos was politic for the Catholic church, which went to any length to discourage popular cults around stones. Stories of origin at the hands of giants were trumped by the Virgin Mary, after an alleged appearance of Notre-Dame des Cieux, who popped up here one day with the baby Jesus. Or was it quite another virgin, Saint Victoria, who chased a man-eating dragon away from its lair in the boulders and was later buried in the same cave herself? That seems much more fitting a legend for the setting.

There is stunning surprise and remarkable beauty here, but this is also the 'top' chaos in Brittany by virtue of accessibility, with close proximity to parking, bars and restaurants in the village. It is the most popularised of all, dis-served by banal recent noticeboards which do little to explain the history of the site or the geological origins of the chaos itself. Huelgoat is a place that prides itself on legends, even if some may barely predate the 1970s revival of Celticism, and has little truck with more rigorous demands of history, a pity as the social and economic development of the town and its natural resources is every bit as interesting as giants, fairies and what may be a tenuous connection with King Arthur. 'Saying doesn't make it so' will never be a popular slogan of tourism, but legends can be fake news too.

Huelgoat granite is grey, from bright to dark, with largish crystals thanks to a very lengthy cooling period of magma and very slow erosion on exposure of the surface. This is contrary to the earliest scientific thoughts on the subject, as Alexander von Humboldt, who visited here in 1813 and would found the Society of Geography in Paris in 1821, was of the opinion that the rocks were formed by the bubbling out and solidifying of molten material pushed up through other layers (like toothpaste spurting from a tube, rather the way the pillow lavas to be seen at Lostmarc'h on the Crozon peninsula arrived). Incorrect as a theory, but it could almost be adopted as a legend, the thought of those enormous glowing red bubbles belching out and heaving away... The visuals and drama of story are both there. Set it up against the tale of the rocks of the Mare aux Sangliers in the forest being grey lumps because they were petrified baby boar covered in ash from having been hidden in an oven by an old woman trying to cheat a couple of saints, and my money's on the bubbles.

The chaos of Huelgoat was very nearly lost to industrial exploitation. Quarrying up until the beginning of the 20th century led to the extraction and destruction of many stones, and the marks of cutting tools are still to be seen on numerous remaining boulders. Individual rocks of character that are high points for visitors today like The Mushroom and the Trembling Rock (see Chapter 10) with its line of chisel holes are natural phenomena, gradually exposed from their fellows and rendered isolated by this economic imperative. Before that they were lost within the density of the site, a great sea of stones merging with the forest.

The Chaos as it stands today was only saved from complete destruction by an organised campaign involving many well-known figures from the creative world, like artist Paul Sérusier, writer Victor Ségalen and folklorist Anatole Le Braz, as well as the Touring Club of France. At the very end of the 19th century, the balance was beginning to tip from local industry in favour of new-fangled tourism. The block of small apartments just above the mill by the lake at the entrance to the Chaos was built in 1904, an annexe to the Hotel de France, to serve this increasing demand, as cycling, fishing, painting as well as general sight-seeing, drew the crowds. More and more it was a destination for English travellers. The great stones were becoming attractive for their own sake, something to be marvelled at and admired, cherished as a crucial part of local tradition, rather than hacked to bits for building projects.

The Trembling Rock has no legend, except for recently generated ones to make up for this deficit, but at least it can provide entertainment (page 182). Arthur's Grotto, considered in the next chapter, and Arthur's Camp combine the legendary hero and his role as a resister of foreign invaders, a theme dear to the hearts of Bretons embittered by French oppression over the centuries. Prosper Merimée, inspector and classifier of historical monuments, came to Huelgoat in 1836 and expressed surprise that the locals 'seemed much more familiar with Caesar than Arthur'. The camp in question is actually an Iron Age hill fort at the top of the forest, excavated by Mortimer Wheeler in 1938. He found evidence of the *murus Gallicus* defence system described by Caesar elsewhere in France. Whether a great battle between Celts and Romans was ever fought here is questionable, but the *oppidum* used the natural defences of huge granite rocks for a defensive inner area in times of trouble.

The Chaos continues in the most beautiful section of the forest from the Gouffre downriver, and here we have the Fairies' Pool, where these ethereal beings sat at night to comb their hair in good siren fashion, and also connection with an important Celtic legend. The story of Dahut and the Breton Atlantis is recorded in Chapter 6, but this princess was also said to have access to the magic forest by way of secret tunnels from the coast to the great stony height above the Gouffre, a chasm where water plunges under the rocks. Here, completely free of her father and his saintly advisors, she was said to take a different lover every night, covering their faces with a mask which turned to an instrument of strangulation when she was finished with them. The servants then hurled their bodies down into the chasm below and the haunting cries to be heard beyond the crash of the water to this day are said to be their spirits still in torment.

For all the enlivenment these stories of giants, fairies and warriors provide for visitors, bringing the natural site into a busy world of action and animation, there remains something profoundly remote, still and arcane about the forest and boulders of Huelgoat. The magic is somewhere elemental, well beyond the reaches of tourist tales.

The **Gorges du Corong** is the most impressive chaos of all. Everyone knows that it was created by the giant Boudedéo emptying his shoe of irritating pebbles. So far, so unoriginal. But this remote and spectacular scene is little celebrated despite its powerful character: it has not been branded (yet) and the setting is enchanting. Part of the special nature of Corong (a bathing-place in Breton), set in a deep gorge, is the effort required to get there and, of course, back. My most cogent experience over various visits has been from starting at the parking of Quelenec between Locarn and Saint Nicodème. Crossing the Landes de Locarn before descending to the river creates an initial impression of wildness that continues down to the stones themselves. Before that, there are two

Gorges du Corong

standing-stones worth seeing. The Menhir de Quelenec, rising from the landscape about 150m beyond the car-park, is also known as *Paotr Saot*, the guardian of the flock, for its air of surveying the surrounding grazing possibilities on this rough moorland. The Menhir des landes de Guellec by contrast is concealed among trees, a delightful warmly shaped stone, probably by natural deterioration rather than intention, but there is something almost human about its curves and recesses.

The moorland walk is dominated by towering pines and gleaming yellow trees of broom in season, with hints of the rocky landscape to come. At the bottom, a narrow earth path descends still further to the chaos itself, initially and deceptively, beside a quiet stream. Soon there are signs of huge rock formations on the hills above: one of them is said to resemble the profile of Anne de Bretagne, the Duchess of Brittany (and twice Queen of France at the end of the 15th century) who has herself entered the legendary world at many points in the Breton tradition, despite being a well-documented historical figure. Beside the path is an old wall, variously dated anywhere between the 12th and the 19th century, and said by some to have been built in a single night by *lutins* (elves). It may have been part of an enclosure for hunting grounds of the local lords or the dukes of Brittany, as there was once a ducal château at Kerbennès, known in the 17th century as the *Loge des Lions du Duc*. No trace of lions, but apparently wild horses were captured and trained here for service in the Crusades c1200 by the Templars of the local *commanderie*, under the aegis of La Feuillée in Finistère.

The deep descent contributes to this exceptional chaos. The river in the bottom of the gorge is a tributary of the Hyères, also known as the *rivière du Follezou*, or river of mad people. There is certainly a little natural craziness in evidence all around. When the water levels are high, the crash and roar can be heard echoing up from the narrow chasm on approach. Its origins lie in a fault line and the resulting valley is narrow, appearing more so with the wooded cover on both sides. Forget calm stretches of low flat stones gently lapped by delicate water: this chaos is monumental, like excessive fortifications, an enormous structure barring the passage of the river, throwing out its own challenge. Ultimately without success, as water trumps stone every time in the end. In winter surges rip out from every crevice, like a hurtling flood crashing down the slippery slope.

From the first moment of encounter here, the sheer concentration of stones has a forceful impact, but it's important to go right to the far end of the chaos to get a real idea of the scale and the gradient. From the bottom a veritable, almost impenetrable, citadel rears up overhead. It is one of the most impressive natural sights in Brittany. It seems almost like a fortified zone, quite unlike the other places in this chapter, with the stones packed together and stacked up in such a mass that it is hard to imagine any airy emptiness in between. The relation of stone to stone is predominant, throwing out the notion of compression, with rocks squeezed into an unforgiving space. Steep sides account for this, giving the impression not so much of tumbled as fallen hard. Even the air tastes of stones. Corong retains the essence of chaos more than any other: it is simply unforgettable in a competitive field.

The **Chaos du Gouët**, south of Saint Brieuc, is actually pluralised into Les Chaos, because a long stretch of the water is adorned with granite boulders of many shapes and sizes, and just when you think it's all over, another section festooned with rocks appears. Like Mardoul it feels impressive but not over-dramatic, a simple natural site, the valley deep but wider and flatter than at Corong. It's a sort of 'pick your own' in terms of story, with little beyond traditional Devil and Virgin associations for certain rocks.

It feels as if the stones are their own story, and the actual site is refreshingly free of information panels. Rumour has it that rites of the Celtic god Lug were once celebrated here for the harvest in early August. The rocks are grouped here and there rather than solidly massed, and many are small, so the water has plenty of room to dance or spread in pools even in the dryness of summer. The atmosphere then is all soft and green, with towering trees and lush foliage tempering the river edges and obscuring much of the rocky walls holding it all together. In winter there is fluvial turmoil to be had and far fewer rocks on display above the waterline. Old postcards from the early 20th century show the valley almost denuded of trees, revealing craggy hillsides and presenting a decidedly different ambience.

Three menhirs in the vicinity suggest that this special site was known and valued in the neolithic period. The Menhir de l'Hopital in Plaine-Haute and La Roche Longue at Saint Julien are both 5m beauties of porphyroid granite commonly found in the Quintin area, whilst the little Menhir de Prétoquis (1.85m) shows what dolerite can do for effect. Perhaps the raised stones even marked the spot for passing visitors, way-marking at least as effective as some of the modern signalling, because this chaos is not so easy to find. Or perhaps they paid tribute to the life-giving water of the river Gouët, which rises near Kerchouan in the commune of Saint Bihy and flows out 46 kilometres later at the port of Légué into what is now the Bay of Saint-Brieuc. Although some tales have grown up of Chouan hideouts in Revolutionary times from this hamlet name, it seems that the derivation is really from Jupiter (*Jovis* leading to *Jouan* and then a simple mistranslation).

How often simple distortions lead to stories! Saint Brieuc himself arrived here from Great Britain in the 5th century and, observing the water's iron-bearing redness, named it Ar Gwad (river of blood), a word that morphed into Gouët over time. A more traumatic version possibly deriving from long local memory has it that Viking blood shed at a nearby battle site during Alain Barbetorte's 9th century struggle against the incomers stained the waters of the river. The remains of a Viking camp can be seen at Péran, not far away.

For such a secluded location, this stretch of the river has seen a lot of human action and exploitation. There were once eleven mills, the remains of two of which are in good evidence, mostly for grain but also to facilitate processes of the cloth industry, which thrived around Quintin. A surviving mill-stone can be seen in the water near the bridge of stone slabs, which is raised on square piles across the flow. Quarrying also took place in situ as marks on various rocks demonstrate, and there was some small-scale farming activity carried out in steep fields or where the valley broadened into pasture. It is hard to imagine people living and working here now, as the long descent by sunken ways and luxuriantly free vegetation at the bottom gives a sense of isolation from civilisation. It is certainly hard to believe that the departmental capital with its torturous traffic is only a short distance away.

Five different versions of chaos, and there are many others to be found in secret spots around Brittany. To sum up their nature, you can't know chaos. It retains a wild, primeval spirit, slipping from the grasp of familiarisation. Stories don't tame it. Names will never hurt it. The lonelier the location, the more exposed its unsettling identity. A subcutaneous fear lingers around those eerie living spaces protected by the stones, something that escapes scientific analysis. For me it demonstrates best a simple sense of sequence that underpins both history and geography. Chaos is part of the long view. This is what happens.

2 STONY WORDS

The Breton language is a hymn to the countryside, reflecting the close relationship of a rural people and their land. Words describe, express form, location, give spatial awareness and direction, pointing up landmarks and features that bind individuals to their locality and their history. A lump of stone called the *plueg Sant Erwan* (the pillow of Saint Yves) at Trédrez conjures up the entire personage of the patron saint of Brittany, who preferred an austere life of deprivation to home comforts, preaching in the fields and meditating on the cliff-top in this lonely parish of his early career. The jumbled remains of a neolithic burial place in the Forêt de Paimpont are called the *Tombeau des Anglais*, the tomb of the English, an echo of the widespread devastation wrought by the Hundred Years War in Brittany and in particular the Battle of Mauron in 1352, suggesting an early origin for the story, but thousands of years out in terms of the origins of the stones themselves. Toponyms enshrine a cultural history where words matter, and the oral tradition preserves this largesse.

In Basse Bretagne, the Breton-speaking west of Brittany, the basic word for stone is *men*, with variants *min* or *maen*. In the form *menec* it defines a characteristic, a stony place such as Menec and Petit Menec at Carnac where there are rows of menhirs (long stones). The region Pays du Mené in Côtes d'Armor is from *menez* or mountain, so its other appellation Monts du Méné is a tautology. Four forms appear in different areas: *moné*, *mené*, *miné* and *mané (*the latter in the name of a famous hill, *Maneguen,* the White Mountain, in Morbihan*)*. The Black Mountains south of the Aulne basin show the plural in Menezioù Du, or Montagnes Noires in French. From a distance this range appears considerably more impressive than the statistics of their actual measurements warrant.

Petit Menec

Our Breton highpoints are more mountains of memory than dazzling heights, part of the Armorican *massif* with the **Monts d'Arrée (Menez Are)** in central Finistère providing not only the topmost crests at a little under four hundred metres above sea level, but also a wealth of stony vocabulary and legend. This range was long ago as high as the Alps and has held onto a lofty atmosphere with its desolate spaces, moors and craggy schist/quartzite crests. *Roc'h*, or French *roc* and *roche* are all used for distinctive stony places like Roc'h Trévezel, one of the iconic highpoints of the Monts d'Arrée, and the highest of them all, but less well-known, Roc'h Ruz, the Red Rock. This was established at 385m as the pre-eminent point of Brittany in 2010. It looks like a little pimple on the horizon, facing north to the right of the communications mast that tops the ridge of little peaks.

Menez Mikael or Mont-Saint-Michel-de-Brasparts is the most famous hill in this area, thanks to the little chapel that dominates the skyline from all around. At the foot, on a plateau above the bogs of the Yeun Elez and the reservoir, a neolithic alignment of dozens of stones is named *An Eured Vein* (The Stone Wedding Party), where the plural of stone *mein* is mutated. The story of its name is from a band of drunken revellers turned to stone by a priest for lack of respect as their paths crossed on the moor late at night. He was taking the sacrament to a dying parishioner, they were returning home from a marriage knees-up and refused to make way, mocking the holy man for his outraged dignity. Nearby is Roc'h Kleger, the Rocky Rock (which appears in another form in the village names Cléguer and Cléguerec in Morbihan). The village of Le Mengleuz (quarry) near Plouneour-Menez a few kilometres to the north witnesses a small-scale economic activity in this area of poor soil, where thick schist roof-tiles were important products. The name *Krag/crag* is also found, for example in the Landes du Cragou (plural), one of the least known ridges to the east of the main crests.

North of the Monts d'Arrée, a remarkable paleolithic site is called Roc'h Toul (see p.46), which signifies a cave (or *grotte* in French) as it means literally a rock with a hole in it, although *toul(l)* can also mean a dip in the ground, hence a valley (also called *traon*). The *Toul ar laerien or* Thieves' Lair, 500m north of the Gorges du Corong, is a great mass of rock with a cave used in the 19th century as a refuge of well-known horse thieves who butchered their prey on a large stone table… Another word for a cavernous space is *mougeo*, which in fact describes a wonderful *allée couverte* at Mougau Bihan near Commana (see p.60).

The word *car* (rock) is pre-Celtic and then *carn* / *karn* (a pile of stones) is found in old Irish, Welsh and Breton, often in association with a burial mound, like **Île Carn (Enez Karn)** off the north coast of Finistère. Here there is a large tumulus covering three dolmens, the earliest parts of the monument dating back to 4200BC. Prolific folklorist Paul Sebillot (1843-1918) recounts a gruesome story set here about the lord of the island, called Karn, who has horse's ears. To preserve his secret he murders all the young men who come out to shave him, until one has the sense to slit his client's throat before he himself is added to the number of bodies. The name Carnac (first appearing in a document in 1387), and probably from the Gaulish form *Carn-acon,* is a place of stones, and *cairn* a tumulus made up of small stones. *Cal* may also be a derivation, with Breton *kalet* = hard and the French *caillou*, a pebble. Cairn (from Scotland) was an adopted usage from the 19th century.

The names commonly used today for megaliths, *menhir* (standing-stone) and *dolmen* (burial place) were first used for this purpose in the 18th century by Theodore-Malo Corret de La Tour d'Auvergne (a war hero made Premier Grenadier of France by Napoléon), who was born near Carhaix. He was a prolific researcher and writer: when held as a prisoner in England, he produced a dictionary of French and Celtic languages. In 1796 he published *Recherches sur la langue, l'origine et l'antiquités des Celto-Bretons de l'Armorique,* where he used the Breton terms *dolmen* and *menhir* or *minhir*, a created vocabulary for designating the commonest neolithic remains. Dolmen has become a generic word for burial places which have nothing in common with the shape indicated in the name – stone (*men*) table (*dol*), but it is easily understood in the simplest form of uprights and a lintel for the entrance.

A common local word in Breton for standing-stones is *peulven* (stone post = upright) and this can still be seen in place names like Kerampeulven (the village of the standing-stone) outside Huelgoat, which has a particularly fine example. At Kerpeulven (or Kerbelven) in Penvénan, a 4m menhir stands in a private garden, visible from the road. An unusual phenomenon characteristic of southern Finistère is *mein zao* (singular *men zao, min zao*) or *pierres debout* in French, upright raised stones used in a line to mark boundaries, or form enclosures or even construct walls of cottages, a striking feature to be seen in the area of Nevez and Pont Aven. The oldest street in Nevez is lined by 112 upright stones, more than 2 metres high. This distinctive practice of the 17th and 18th centuries is now designated as protected architectural heritage.

Bre (or *Bri*) is another word for mountain or hill, like the distinctive pinnacle in the town of Lannion called Brélévenez or 'hill of joy'. Here seemingly endless flights of wide steps lead up to the dominant glory of the Église de la Trinité, which retains evidence of its Romanesque origins and has a striking porch in pink granite flanked by two jutting columns. Local tradition maintains it was founded by the Knights Templar. But of all the stories conjured by stony words and the places they describe, the most dramatic and nuanced must be that of the Mené-Bré and the infamous villain Conomor. This is one of the traditional seven sacred hills of Brittany, and all retain their lofty names: Menez Hom, Menez Mikael (Mont-Saint-Michel-de-Brasparts), Mané Guen, Menez or Mont Bel

Air, Mont Dol, and Mont St-Michel (which we all know is Breton but for the sneaky, or rather snaky, behaviour of the Couesnon river).

Mené Bré (301m), an eminence with commanding views of the Trégor in north Côtes d'Armor, was the scene of a 6th century confrontation between the Dark Age warlord Conomor and his enemies. Frankly, who needs a shadowy King Arthur when Brittany has this extraordinary figure, weaving history and legend into a significant pattern so indelibly indicative of its time. He is surely the most intriguing figure in a highly competitive world of legendary personages, combining an historical role in the developing state that would one day form Brittany, and a reputation as the Breton Bluebeard. He has become an emblematic representative of the turbulence and uncertainty of Armorica after the departure of the Romans, and the earliest interactions with the rising empire of the Franks.

Conomor, born in the first half of the 6th century, probably came from Cornwall to settle in Brittany. (Some see him as King Mark himself, working from evidence of the Tristan stone found at Golant which bears the form of his name Cunomorus). If he once lived in Caerhays near modern Megavissey, he perhaps gave the name to Carhaix (although this is more likely derived from its position as an important crossroads), for he was the Count of Poher, the area south and east of this town, in the former territory of the Osismes tribe. He is also associated with the Forêt de Quénécan (now on the southern shore of Lac de Guerlédan) and the Forêt de Carnoët. In the historical record he is mentioned by Gregory of Tours, a contemporary author, as a Breton count, and he also appears in a later *Life of Saint Hervé* as a prefect of the King of the Franks, showing their early interest in control over areas in the far west. Some think Conomor had a brief in this context to oversee maritime affairs and coastal defences between Britain and Brittany.

He was a bellicose, ambitious character, a ruthless leader with expansionist tendencies. He married the widow of the King of Domnonée to expand his power base in the north, and after her death took another wife, Tréphine, daughter of the Count of Vannes. This is where the Bluebeard legend creeps in, as Conomor is said in popular tradition to have married numerous times and murdered his wives to avoid a prophecy that his son would kill him. This young bride was no exception and he decapitated her when she became pregnant. Amazingly she survived (as we'll see later on) and managed to give birth to a son, Trémeur, in hiding. Years later Conomor succeeded in hunting the young boy down and cutting off his head too (see p.161). The church in Carhaix is dedicated to this child martyr and a western tower statue shows him holding his own head in his hands (see also Chapter 9).

Conomor's dastardly deeds and his brutal expansionism eventually caught up with him. In 548, a council of religious leaders, including the seven bishops of Brittany, Gildas, a long-term opponent, and blind Saint Hervé, a leading monastic figure, was called to meet on Mene Bré, and the tyrant himself summoned to appear before them. Hervé was late getting to the venue with his guide the young Guiharan, but a stuffy church figure who chivvied at hanging around for some old hermit, got struck down by blindness for his lack of respect. Luckily Saint Hervé was not the sort to take unnecessary offence, on this occasion anyway, and on arrival released him from his pains.

After an acrimonious confrontation at this gathering, Conomor was officially excommunicated, but he remained defiant to the last, swearing revenge. There is a wonderful stained glass window in Pedernec church dramatically portraying this scene on Mene Bré. His patron Childebert, Emperor of the Franks, finally heeded the advice of Saint Samson that Conomor deserved his punishment and agreed to release Judual, the tyrant's stepson, from the court in

Paris where he was being held nominally as a guest, but without freedom of movement. Back in Brittany Judual raised forces to face Conomor and was victorious in a savage battle fought near Le Relec in the Monts d'Arrée. The prophecy sort of came true after all, with single combat between father and stepson, and Conomor's dynamic ambition was finally brought to an end. A sepulchre for the fallen (*releg* = burial ground) gave the place its name, well known today for the Cistercian Abbaye du Relec.

This story, whatever its degree of historicity, reflects the issues and rivalries of its time. The well-established Church of Rome in eastern Brittany, the Celtic hermit from western Brittany where the arrival of holy men and women from Great Britain was in full swing, as well as the rivalries of small militarised territories and the defence of economic resources to support power. It also indicates the issue of relations with the Franks and their influence on the development of a nascent Breton state which was to come to fruition only in the 9th century when separate power blocks united in the face of former allies now become enemies. Saint Hervé stayed to found a hermitage on Mené Bré, and to this day an ancient chapel in his honour stands in this dominant position with its panoramic views. There has also been a recent controversy about the placing of a permanent giant statue of the saint near the chapel. The Pardon celebrating the saint's day is on the third Sunday in June, but the site is better known now for its horse festival on 15th August, a tradition started by the monks of Bégard in the 12th century.

The geographical position of Mont Dol and Mont Saint Michel in eastern Brittany rather than the Breton-speaking west, is reflected in their names. Here Gallo was the local language from the 11th century, its roots reaching back to the Romanisation of the region from the first century. It is classed as a Romance language, one of the *langues d'oïl* with influences of French, Breton and (on the coast)

Chapelle Saint Hervé, Mené Bré

Norse. *Mont* appears in place-names for a hill more than a hundred times in Ille-et-Vilaine, such as Monthault (see p.186) and it can also indicate a fortified place, as in Montfort. *Roche* is also used in this context, like Rochefort-en-Terre. La Grée-Saint-Laurent shows the use of *grée* for a rocky hill. In Haute-Bretagne the French *pierre* for stone is often used, but sometimes it could be referencing the personal name instead. The frequent appearance of the name *La Perrière* in this area indicates quarrying activity.

Granite is perceived as the dominant stone of Brittany, even if the picture is not quite as simple as that. In French there is a difference between *granit* and *granite* to note in passing, both derived from the Italian *granito* for a hard rock. *Granit* is used in this sense today in the practical business of quarrying and architecture, but scientifically *granite* indicates a stone made up of some combination of feldspar, mica and quartz. Despite the common perception of a preponderance of general grey in Brittany, there is no such thing as a single type but many localised examples varying in ingredients to produce a great range of colours and textures. The Côte de Granit Rose is an obvious example, but not far from there on the north coast is a blue/green stone for which Locquirec was well-known, and the light grey of Huelgoat is familiar from the huge boulders there that form a major tourist attraction.

Metamorphic schist also has major colour variation, from the sombre hue of the Monts d'Arrée (where it is known as *maen glas*, blue stone) to a strong purple (a shade known as *lie du vin* – 'dregs of wine' in French) in the area south-west of Rennes, shown to perfection in the extraordinarily evocative Château de Trécesson near Paimpoint, reached by a causeway over a lake. This medieval fortress has attracted many legends, particularly of ghosts from a headless priest to a White Lady, the phantom of a young bride buried alive by her brothers, who appears on the roof of the château on the nights of a full moon. Another bright stone is the Pierre de Logonna (also called Pierre du Roz) from western Finistère around Logonna-Daoulas, a fine building stone, whose gorgeous ochre tones can be seen in the architecture of towns like Landerneau and Le Faou.

Last mention must go to the dark kersanton, a unique fine-grained stone, like but not actually granite, and the only one taking its name from Breton toponymy, specifically a village on the Rade de Brest. Here it must have been exploited as early as the 12th century from its appearance at the Abbaye de Daoulas, and the last quarry closed in the first years of the 21st century. This material has been used extensively in architecture and sculpture, being easy to work but also highly resistance to erosion. On a large scale it features on the lighthouses of Eckmühl in Penmarc'h and Île Vierge on the north coast. More immediately visual in religious context, it forms a striking contrast with lighter stones, for example in the monumental calvary at Plougastel-Daoulas, with the base formed in yellow Logonna blocks, topped by 182 figures carved from kersanton. In the hands of a master craftsman like Roland Doré (c1585-1663), the possibility of exquisite detailing emerges in memorably delicate statuary, like Saint John on the porch at Saint-Thégonnec. The sombre hue of kersanton also made it a natural choice for war memorials and other funerary monuments.

Finally it must be noted that Breton place-names have many forms, and maps may offer variants which can be confusing. Actually finding a stone in Brittany is often half the fun. But just think of those wretched French mapmakers in the 18th century, knowing little or no Breton and trying to make sense of the topography. *Tossenn* (*tosten*, *tuchen*, *dossen*, *dosten*) means a prominent point or sometimes a tumulus. A famous hill in the Monts d'Arrée is called Tuchenn Gador, with a distinctive natural rocky formation on the summit, a bit like a throne (*kador* = chair) from a distance. But *tuchenn* was a step too far for French ears, and they went for simple euphony instead, labelling the spot Signal de Toussaines, akin to Toussaint, All Saints, which is still to be found on some maps today. I suppose it seemed safe enough in the land of a thousand saints, even if there is no connection in reality. What's in a name after all?

3 Cover

Stone has provided refuge of all sorts since the beginning of human settlement. Caves were inner and outer places, offering shelter, defensive positions and look-out points. They may have been associated with burial from the earliest times. Later constructed chambers for the dead or for ritual purposes recreated this notion of the dark space, a durable protection, the safety of the womb, especially in areas where geology was less giving in that form of terrain. Without natural caves, man could create a facsimile. Conversely they were also perceived, by virtue of their hidden interiors, as places of danger and threat. This idea, together with the often allied notion of stashing precious things in secret places, gave rise to many legends featuring wild creatures and treasure-seeking. Cover and concealment are both crucial tools of survival, for the living and for monuments of the dead.

The story begins on the sharp slopes above the river Penzé where one of the earliest natural shelters used by man in Brittany is located. **Roc'h Toul**, literally the rock with a hole in it, lies covertly on private land at Luzec, in the commune of Guiclan. The steep and unmarked approach offers glimpses and then a sudden confrontation with the huge lustrous twin-peaked outcrop which houses the grotto. This towering sandstone mass looms above the narrow opening, an irregular slash in the overhanging rock, with the cave itself divided into two parts. The first is a large chamber (11.5m deep x 4m at the greatest extent), its floorspace broken up by a group of small rocks in the centre. It ends in a ledge about 1m high, with large blocks further obscuring the raised entrance to the second chamber (barred), a much narrower tunnel tapering back more than thirty metres into the hillside. A protected bat colony is established in the inner section, one reason why there is no overt encouragement for visitors.

This stone space has an unchanging atmosphere that tells something of its early inhabitants. Looking out from the entrance, which is shielded by a massive outside extension of the north wall, the cave seems to hang in suspension riding a sea of trees, a concealed refuge of rough and fissured surfaces, stained green and brown by natural process. It maintains a sense of being tucked away, right inside the hill, secured from the stresses and dangers of the outer world. The site is not well-known, which doubtless contributes to the vibrant energy that lingers right into the innermost folds of this cavern. It was first discovered and excavated in 1868 by a Docteur Le Hir from Morlaix. He found flint and quartzite tools, scrapers and cutting implements typical of Mesolithic occupation c10,000BC and fragments of charcoal in the second chamber.

One or more small groups of people inhabited this place over an extended period of time around 12,000 years ago. They looked out at dawn from the entrance over the valley, alert for unwelcome visitors or welcome prey. They went down to the river for fish and into the forest to hunt. Housed in stone, they used other stone to create implements to make the practicalities of life easier. They lit fires and sheltered from the weather underneath this density of rock, which enclosed and framed their precarious lives for short or longer periods, offering a consistent fixed point in semi-nomadic existence, the essential value of a roof over the head, as important now as then.

This is the real story, but a tale based on the evocative siting and interior of Roc'h Toul was recorded by Breton teacher and writer Yves Miossec (1907-2001). It evokes the great love of a certain young noble of Kerfaven for the daughter of another noble from Saint-Thégonnec. What prevented him from declaring his feelings was the rather off-putting stipulation of her father that any serious suitor for his daughter's hand must enter the cave of Roc'h Toul and find the treasure buried at the very bottom, guarded by a terrible dragon. This was enough to deter most prospective husbands, but a couple of bolder souls who had tried to fulfil the condition never returned. However, the *chevalier* of Kerfaven was so in love he decided to make the attempt, taking the precaution of a companion, the miller of Luzec, to help him in his quest. This man was said to have certain magical powers, which made him a useful ally, and he accepted the nobleman's proposition willingly, not surprisingly considering he happened to know that the treasure could be had if the dragon was offered a human sacrifice. This seemed a perfect opportunity for him to provide a victim and take the treasure for himself.

They set off on the expedition. The miller brought two big sacks with him, the noble carried a spade, his rosary and a little cross. When they arrived at the cave, all began well. The outer chamber was still and quiet as they passed, climbing over the stony division at the back and into the more confined space beyond. The young man started digging into the floor of the cave, and soon found a wooden box with rusty metal hinges. Inside was a treasure of gold coins and precious stones beyond their wildest dreams. After a moment of disbelief at their easy triumph, they crammed the two bags full of jewels and began to leave the passage, struggling under the weight of their booty. But all at once a great roar filled the cavern, so immense that the huge rocks themselves trembled and shook. It was the dragon, splaying green flames from its jaws. The miller stepped forward boldly, holding up a secret magic talisman. 'Look at this young man,' he said, gesticulating towards his companion. 'His tender flesh is all yours!' The dragon swung at once towards the nobleman, who, despite his fear, raised the little cross in the face of the monster. It veered away as if struck, shifting instead towards the miller, crushing the life from him with the enormous weight of its carcass. Thanking God for his reprieve, the young man dragged the treasure from the cave and went home to claim his bride.

This folktale reflects the ominous appearance of the cavern that may well have instilled fear in the local inhabitants, providing the basis of a story of danger and bravery, an irony with regard to the place of safety it actually provided for those within, in times when settled communities did not exist. But it tells nothing of journey, that steep descent, river crossing and final climb to the raised entrance, the sense of arrival in a place anchored in lost time. The grotto remains largely unchanged from its earliest form, although the immediate environment has been transformed just in the years I've known it by a denuding of trees on the surrounding hillside and a return to the natural flora of the *landes*. This has opened up the aspect but done nothing to expose the concealed opening in the rock-face, which is reached by a short steep scramble. Actually finding the location brings a sense of achievement these days.

Roc'h Toul is a place of simple reality, which has guarded its sense of enduring authenticity. There could not be a greater contrast between this isolated, unvisited site and Arthur's Grotto, another raised cave which lies in the full glare of tourism all year round, on an easy walking path through the forest of Huelgoat. Roc'h Toul has an eternal flavour, a lasting vestige of human experience from pre-history, reinforced by the remoteness of the location. Still more ancient man than modern visitor. More history than folklore.

The hiding of treasure in a cave is a common motif of the latter, and many megaliths were believed to be repositories of hidden wealth. But some exceptional sites have attracted the idea of great men in waiting, their bodies lying in frozen moratorium until the moment when they'll rise again. It's the King Arthur syndrome. The notion that he never died from his wounds on the battlefield but lies somewhere awaiting reanimation by events leads to associations like **Arthur's Grotto** in Huelgoat (or *La Grotte d'Artus* if you prefer a pseudo-medievalism that is probably the product of 1970s tourist promotion or an interpretation deriving from the Celtic word for bear). But leaving aside the grandiose claim, this place is a powerfully telluric spot, rather spoilt by the heroic connection. It is a shallow cavern high above a river stuffed with fallen boulders, surrounded by trees. There is not at all the same sense of permanence that emanates from Roc'h Toul. The classic signs of degeneration are already there in the lines deep in the granite: one day the cave will be no more than an open space and its rocks an addition to the chaos down below. The interior is small and the hillside above can be seen through gaps between the stones. It is more a recess in a pile of granite boulders than a proper cave, but nevertheless a forcefully atmospheric place, reached by stone steps, the height above the path emphasising its singular character.

This site is a fine example of how giving something a name shapes its identity and people's perception of what they see. I have experimented with groups and individuals of all ages there, covering the sign and asking people to give their initial impression on looking up at the high, dark mouth surrounded by huge stones. What do they say? It's a lair. For a dragon or a bear. Maybe the home of a pack of wolves. It's scary. A monster certainly lived there, or a giant. It must be a treasure trove. What about a hermit's refuge? Never has anyone suggested that perhaps some hero lies buried there waiting for a national crisis to reawaken and save his country. (Although the way things are now, that aspiration may soon be added to the choices.) When Jacques Cambry visited in 1795 he was told not of the legendary king, but of demons guarding a treasure here, *feux follets* (will-o'-the-wisps) that shot through the air like fiery

COVER

Arthur's Grotto, Huelgoat

sparks, sending blood-curdling screams echoing down the valley at night. Now that's more like it.

On climbing the steps to the entrance and penetrating the interior, even chatty people usually fall silent. There is something intense but withdrawn here, a suppressed energy, mysterious way beyond a presentation that is banal in comparison. Despite the frequency of footfall – during the first pandemic summer when Huelgoat was completely overwhelmed by visitors seeking the health-giving effect of 'forest bathing', huge queues formed on the path below – some sense of depth and resonance endures, but it is in the stone itself, drawing on time millions of years before the Arthur industry got underway to obfuscate its intrinsic value.

On the subject of famous men syndrome, the thorny question of **Merlin's 'tomb'** plays out in interesting fashion in Brittany where caves are concerned. Of course the **Forêt de Paimpont**, one of the most beautiful natural areas in Brittany (with no need for all the hype), which styles itself Brocéliande and makes ambitious Arthurian claims, must contain such a seminal site, a place where visitors can pay tribute to the ultimate magician and indeed call on his powers to this very day for help in a variety of situations. They have been quite flexible with their associations there, transferring the Arthurian Valley of No Return from one spot to another after a new factory rather spoilt the legendary notion of the first. But the problem for Merlin's resting place is geological. A strong tradition places Merlin's tomb in a cave (a solid representation of the 'circles of air' in which Viviane ensnared him), but there are no caves to fit the bill in this terrain of red schist. This is why the astonishingly unimpressive Merlin's tomb in the forest is the scant remnant of a megalith, just a couple of stones, now surrounded by planting and fencing to intensify the site, where people can shove their messages and vows, written on scruffy pieces of paper, into the cracks of the rocks. It's hard to see how someone can be contained inside something with no interior. This is the most forced and artfully created artificial association of them all and it surprises, if not disappoints, many visitors, who are expecting a cave. Or it provides amusement. Merlin himself can probably see the funny side of some stumpy rocks as his eternal resting place.

But he has other options in Brittany where he is associated with imprisonment in various grottoes. There's one at Le Quillio, a dark lair under huge rocks, and another with its feet in the waters of the Blavet river at Plounévez-Quintin. But my favourite, which blows the others out of the water if you want a sense of place fitting its story, is on the steep slope of **Mont Dol**, near Dol-de-Bretagne. It requires something of an effort to reach, a climb down from the summit of this mysterious hill, and the way is completely unmarked, but once seen, never forgotten. There is a sinister air to the towering sheer rock-face and low black entrance to the cave, a real notion of fearsome incarceration, the sense of being surrounded by impenetrable walls. A prison to be proud of, and let's face it, surely it would take quite a strongbox to keep Merlin inside?

There are powerful claims for this area (Dol-Combourg-Bécherel) to be the original inspiration for Brocéliande, if we must have a literal association for a literary creation. The ancient forest there, of which parts remain, was called Quokelunde in the *Roman du Mont Saint Michel* by Guillaume Saint-Par, a 12th century monk from the great abbey. (And it is worth remembering that the ancestors of Geoffrey of Monmouth, who could be said to have generated the whole Arthur saga, were from Dol-de-Bretagne.) Certainly Lancelot's origins seem centred on this area and he is regarded as the 'Breton contribution' to the Arthurian stories. It conforms to criteria in the oldest sources that Brocéliande is in the Marches of Brittany and near the sea, details quite inapplicable to the Forêt de Paimpont. This latter forest, however, benefited from a clever marketing initiative in the early 19th century, which was to be a decisive factor in its reputation and popularity today.

The story of the construction of its image is almost a folktale in its own right. Not long after the Paris publication in 1812 of Auguste Creuzé de Lesser's epic poem *La table ronde* led to huge interest in the world of Arthur and his knights, Blanchard de la Musse from Montfort-sur-Meu on the edge of the Forêt de Paimpont, with his friend Maître Poignard, a local judge, began to search their area and make direct associations with places in the stories. Hence Merlin's tomb of stone but no cave. It was the best they could do. These enterprising polymaths were successful in laying the foundations of the great tourist coup that today dominates the Arthurian scene in Brittany. Meanwhile Mont Dol, a site of mystery and magic if ever there was one, quietly contains its many potential Arthurian connections and remains somewhat overshadowed by the proximity of international star Mont St Michel, with which it has always been linked in pilgrimage. There is also some historical evidence for the Holy Grail at Dol-de-Bretagne too, but that's another story altogether...

Moving from natural shelter into the realm of constructed cover, the great **cairn of Barnenez** in Plouezoc'h to the north of Morlaix, may be the earliest monument in Europe. The scale and care of construction suggest that it was exceptional from conception. It is a unique and haunting site, even though the environment is much changed since it was built. There were two phases in a rough east/west orientation: an initial line of five tombs, the small round or polygonal chambers accessed by long corridors dates from about 4700BC and it was followed by a unit of six further tombs between 4300BC and 3900BC. The cairn of small stones enclosing the whole structure is 80m long and 30m wide in its restored state, both dominating and blending into the landscape as the first phase was near the top of the promontory and the second had to be adapted by a stepped structure to fit the slope. The monument was not conceived as a lone statement, but another cairn on the site was destroyed in the 20th century (see Chapter 12), leaving scant trace on the ground today. The damage inflicted at this time also revealed the rear of several chambers (the front entrances are blocked): some have the superb drystone *tholos* roof construction, in contrast with the large capstones used in others. The whole hillside of the site is enclosed today and charges a fee for visitors, a rare situation in Brittany, reflecting its importance.

The position was presumably chosen for visibility, a low rise above the river plain that is now concealed by higher sea levels. The promontory is on a basis of schist and dolerite, with the latter stone used to build the first cairn, the use of local stone underlining the connection of people and place. The second phase of development was determinedly different, with granite brought from Île Sterec 2km away. Both reflect the developing processing of stone beyond small tools, learning to select, transport and refine for lasting structure. The prototype of the cave is well advanced already on this site, even into multiplicity. From the direction of the rising sun to the destination of after-life far away westwards over the water, the monument, with its size and shape like an ocean-going vessel, seems to tell of both life and death.

Another step forward seen in this early construction was the creation of megalithic art, presumably both decorative and symbolic. Five uprights were found to have carvings, although they are not so easy to interpret: a square with spiky hair may be an idol's head, handled U-shapes may be horns, wiggly lines may be snakes, something that might be a bow, and some clearly depicted triangular hand axes. Very recent studies in one tomb show that paint in the colours of black and red was a further enhancement of the dark inner space of the cairn. We don't know for whom these embellishments were intended: the dead or certain living beings who may have been permitted to enter the passage graves for some undefined ritual purposes. It is also impossible to say whether the subjects depicted indicate useful objects for some future after-life or represent the values of the society that built the monument, items of significance to the deceased in their lifetimes.

The technological achievement of this megalith reflects a high skill level and societal confidence, as well as the manpower and organisation required to bring the stone to the site and gradually raise the cairn from nothing to a substantial presence which has remarkably stood the test of time. It is a form of productivity, tribute to the dead and expression of the continuity of the living.

The builders were the first exploiters of the land, discovering the benefits of agriculture and fixed settlement. This changed man's relationship with his natural environment, initiating ideas of possession and ownership that set the scene for visible manifestation in monuments, probably staking a claim on territory. The cairn speaks of roots and permanence achieved through skilful labour, making a deliberate impact on landscape and erecting a lasting memorial for the people who built it, as well as those who were buried there.

That usage continued over a long period is indicated in the finds, from excavations by Pierre-Roland Giot (Director of the *Antiquités de Bretagne*) in 1956 and 1968. These include pottery, flint tools and dolerite polished axes (from Plussulien in Côtes d'Armor) dating from the early Neolithic, flint blades from the late Neolithic and a copper dagger and arrowhead from the Copper Age. In one of the dolmens, decomposed vegetal remains were analysed to show wheat, barley, peas and sorrel dating from the medieval period, although they give no indication of what the monument would have been used for then, except perhaps basic cover, which is, after all, one quiet story that Barnenez has to tell us.

Smaller megalithic tombs are found in their hundreds all over Brittany, with the simplest based on the entrance of two uprights and a lintel, like a stone table or dolmen. The shape and construction developed as time went on, from simple corridor graves to the dolmen in a tapering V shape and then the passage grave or *allée couverte*, which appeared c3000BC. Some were intentionally covered with earth mounds or cairns, others may have been designed to stand exposed to view. A surrounding enclosure of smaller stones, as if marking a precinct, was not uncommon. Some have carved decoration and some may have been painted. Bones have by no means always been among the finds, although this is perhaps unsurprising in the acidic soil found in many parts of the region. These covered spaces were not necessarily or exclusively for burials. Some may have been accessed by shaman-like figures, serving as dark enclosures for heightened experience, a complete liberation of spirit within physical limitations. The importance of retaining connection with the ancestors may often have been a factor in the usage of the structures. In some places, bones were taken out, presumably for ritual use, and then replaced. Many were clearly re-used and adapted over long swathes of time. The variety of location and configuration is almost endless, so I have chosen just three memorable examples here with very different settings and senses of cover.

The **Dolmen Ti-ar-Boudiged** (Fairies' House) in Brennilis is an exceptional dolmen in V shape, with the entrance at 1.7m gradually widening to the chamber (3.1m) which is marked by a single internal stone 'separation'. The total length of the structure is nearly 15m, and it is edged by a line of stones on each side. The doorway is orientated to the winter solstice. The dolmen is unusual and particularly suggestive in retaining its covering, a thick roof of earth and grass rendering it very much the little 'house of fairies' which its Breton name describes. Or the perfect image of a hobbit

Ti-ar-Boudiged

house, as more contemporary cultural reference would have it. Without any knowledge to put it in context, one might easily have jumped to the conclusion that it was a primitive dwelling place for small people, and the step to fairy or elf inhabitants is but a short one. The setting is a peaceful haven (complete with picnic table) with a beautiful beech tree spreading over the tomb. It is possible to spend a long time in and around the monument without interruption at most times of year.

The legendary name suggests *lutins* or elves as the founders, rather than the hard-nosed *korrigans* so well-known in the area, as some claim. It looks like a pretty solid residence for little people, secure and protective. This idea of all kinds of special abodes being built and then inhabited by groups or individuals was common in later folklore. Legends often portray this more 'domestic' perception. One has only to look at further local names for dolmens and passage graves: La Maison de Viviane (Arthurian reference in the Forêt de Paimpont), Ty Sant Denez (the House of Saint Denis at Saint-Gouazec), La Maison du Diable (Home of the Devil), Maison des nains (Gnomes' House, another name for the one in Brennilis), La Loge au loup (Wolf's lodging place at Trédion) or Loch-Korrigan (= Loge, a small round dolmen in Melgven).

The shape and material of many megaliths led to association with habitations rather than tombs. They looked like dwelling places with doorways, walls and roofs, whether any enclosing earthwork was lost or not, with an inner structure often lending itself to the interpretation of 'rooms'. The Dolmen de Kerguntuil at Trégastel not only traditionally gave shelter to a 'fairy spinner' who had extraordinary prowess with the spindle, but was later actually turned into a smithy with a bit of bolstering up for the walls. A postcard from the early 20th century describes the megalith as '*a longtemps servi d'habitation*' (long used as a habitation). Cover and shelter for the living rather than a resting place for the bones or spirits of the dead, the start of a story rather than the end. It was by no means the only one inhabited in historical times. The house theme continues with internal decoration found both spectacularly (as in the cairn on the island of Gavrinis) and modestly in many places on orthostats lining the passage of the tomb and sometimes the chamber itself.

Whichever little people made Brennilis their home, they were said to be in conflict with the giants who lived over the 'mountain' range of the Monts d'Arrée, in a spot that just happens to be the site of one of the finest passage graves (*allée couverte*) of all at **Mougau Bihan**, near Commana. This later version of the dolmen, roughly the same width throughout, has the advantage of broadly retaining its context unchanged since the time of construction c3000BC. That is, if you can ignore the foreground, with a gîte alongside and the crop of maize and bits of farm machinery immediately opposite. Look beyond that and there's a wide marshy valley with chronologically appropriate vegetation, and then the rude rise of the highest hills in Brittany, rough crests of schist apparent now as they would have been after the earliest deforestations in the neolithic period. The alley grave is impressive and remarkably well-preserved, 14m long, divided into an 11m chamber and a small *cella* with dividing stone and no roof, like a little outdoor shrine tagged on to the main event. Five huge capstones cover the body of the tomb.

The glory of this monument, however, are the carvings inside. On the end wall separating the *cella* is a magnificent hafted axe, sadly vandalised with pink spray paint from time to time by some persistent objectors to 'pagan' monuments. Luckily stone is very resilient to such attacks and has the benefit of outlasting pretty much anything modern. The other decoration consists of pairs of raised bumps usually interpreted as goddess' breasts (or maybe just breasts), although I wonder if there is not another explanation, and some implements that may be daggers (like the *poignards à soie* found in Cyprus, blades shaped like a willow-leaf), oars or even winnowing tools. There is open access to the alley grave, so close examination of the designs is possible.

Who were they for, these internal decorations? Surely for someone's eyes and if not the dead, then perhaps living visitors to the tomb. Or simply to enhance the stone to give it more value or power in its protective role, overseeing the sanctity of the tomb? Unfortunately these illustrations to the story of the tombs remain enigmatic, and it is unlikely we will ever fully enter the mindset of the makers.

The breasts motif is widespread in use in Brittany. One of the uprights of the *allée couverte* of Kerguntuil in Trégastel (in the same field as the dolmen mentioned above) has six pairs in a line, an emphatic statement of whatever they actually depict. A rather different configuration also appears quite dramatically at one of the most compelling megalithic sites in Brittany, the **allée couverte de Tressé** (in the Forêt du Mesnil), also known as the **Maison des Fées** or **Feins**. The setting is in a beautiful mixed forest of oak, beech and pine, which once belonged to the famous Saint-Malo corsair Robert Surcouf, for use as a hunting ground, as his family owned a manor house at Le Mesnil des Bois. It is reached by a leafy trail through the forest, which builds up the anticipation of the reveal when the grove containing the monument comes into view. This sight never fails to make my heart beat faster. At 14m long, with 41 stones including 8 roof slabs, it has something of the air of a great lithic monster, with an aliveness that can be startling. One can almost imagine it flexing its muscles under the tumulus that would have covered the original structure.

The chamber was at the northern end, separated by a stone slab. Of those divine bumps, the goddesses' breasts, there were four on each of two stones, one line on the exterior of the stone closing off the chamber and the other on a transversal stone outside this, so the lines were at right-angles to each other. The original site report said the representations were realistic because those on the stone to the side were the pointed breasts of a young girl and the others were the full round breasts of a mother. The opportunity to judge this observation is now lost, as the latter set were vandalised in 1980s and no longer in existence, leaving only hollow orbs to mark their former presence.

The place is often deserted, as it is not really on the way to anywhere and has to be sought out, but it also seems to be a focal point for pagans, as I have arrived a couple of times to find personal rituals in progress, such as processions around the perimeter, laying out sticks on the stones in divinatory patterns, and incantations. Once I waited patiently for an hour for my own (quieter) experience, sitting on a rock in the wood in view but well out of the way of the two women engrossed in their ceremony. But when they'd finished they simply climbed on top of the monument, got out a picnic and began chatting loudly about family problems. They clearly felt themselves in some sort of tune with the stones.

The story attached to this super-site is a wonderfully prosaic tale of neighbourly relations and the priorities of rural life. It also expresses how precarious that life could be. The cow belonging to the fairy owners trespassed on a neighbour's territory and trampled his crops. To make amends the fairies gave the farmer a magical loaf of bread which constantly regenerated itself when eaten. So the family would never starve, an important insurance policy in those unpredictable times. But there was a condition attached to this generous gift: the secret of the loaf's powers must never be revealed to anyone. For many years all went well, with the farmer grateful for his added security. One day, however, he forgot the need for discretion and told someone the history of the unfailing bread. At that very moment, the loaf turned to stone.

Sir Robert Mond, the nickel magnate, who had a Breton wife and various properties in Brittany, was wealthy enough to indulge his passion for archaeology on a grand scale, participating in important excavations in Egypt and being instrumental in setting up a British School of Archaeology in Jerusalem after working in Palestine. He excavated and renovated the megalith in the forest at Tressé in 1931 with the help of Vera Christina Chute Collum, a suffragette and anthropologist, who had firm views on the cosmic cult of the Great Mother and the Eternal Feminine. She wrote a book about their work on this site (where finds included a skeleton, Gallo-Roman pottery fragments showing Iron Age re-use, a necklace, and a bronze coin from the reign of Domitian), with the second part devoted entirely to the divine mother theme. The shape of passage graves can be seen in this context as analogous to the female vagina and uterus, echoing the idea of shelter for the baby in the womb, safe under cover of its mother's body.

Turning to the later enclosure of sacred space for Christian worship leads us to the chapels, churches and cathedrals for which Brittany is well-known, but often these started out as humble oratories or simple retreats for prayer. Few people visit what is one of the most numinous places I have ever experienced, convincing me that spirit of place was a factor in choosing early Christian sites. A few kilometres outside Lanrivoaré (see also p.173) is the **Hermitage of Saint Hervé.** Said to have been the refuge of the blind saint, well away from the strictures of organised religion and a more public profile, it is a place of shelter and seclusion, stone built, earth-topped, maybe once covered by rough reed thatch, set in a grove of beech and chestnut, lively trees that seem to carry voices among their leaves. The wind is loud through the branches, but cut into absolute silence by a single step into the cover of the hermitage. There is a curious fulsomeness about this interior absence of sound, sheered off from the active world outside, a microcosm of meditative space away from rambling thought. It's an empty space seemingly full to the brim with stillness, not even an echo to mark the hollow sound characteristic of natural cover.

Parts of the ruined chapel nearby can be dated to the 10th century and the actual hermitage, in its current stone form, may reach back to the 12th, long after the time of Saint Hervé and his wolf companion, but doubtless housing many other hermits over the centuries. (The Dark Age saints who arrived in such great

Hermitage of Saint Hervé

numbers from Britain from the 5th-7th centuries had to make do with wooden or even rush huts and cabins for their homes and oratories.) The grove is split by a satisfying little stream, and there is a rude *fontaine* decorated with a granite H-shaped stone (for Hervé), which probably came much later from another local chapel. Fragments of Roman pottery have been found around here, suggesting that a villa may have once stood in the vicinity. At times the site, including the hermitage itself, has been overtaken by burgeoning grasses and wild flowers, but it had been recently cleared and tidied on my last visit. Whatever the condition, it is the kind of place that you never want to leave, something I can only associate with the rare combination of stirring spirit and absolute peace.

This need for seclusion and cover in the sense of separation from the outside world raises an interesting paradox about the Breton saints. They came from Great Britain as evangelisers, often tasked by divine visions with the role of missionary in their new land. The west of Brittany was sparsely populated and the land overgrown and neglected since the departure of what Roman administration had existed. Whilst the east already had a well-developed Christian system from the Church of Rome, with bishops established at Nantes and Rennes, things were different elsewhere and paganism was still the order of the day, so both the scope for conversions and new religious organisation were imperative. But many of the 'saints', finding a quiet wilderness, succumbed to the charms of peace and tranquillity, seeking isolated spots to build little oratories and devote themselves to a life of prayer and meditation. Even one of the seven 'founders' of Brittany, Saint Pol, found himself manoeuvred into public and political life in the establishment of a cathedral and town (what is now Saint-Pol-de-Léon), when his personal preference was for a reclusive style of living on the Île de Batz.

When he first arrived on the mainland of the continent, he kept trying to settle down with his few followers in lonely places beside idyllic springs or in beautiful groves. Each time he was driven onwards by a divine messenger, in language, according to his *Vita*, that directly echoes the command given to Vergil's hero in the *Aeneid* when he was shirking his duty to the glorious future of Rome by hanging out with Dido in Carthage. And that's quite a thought-provoking parallel in itself! Saint Pol was not much of a warrior and no woman's lover, although he did persuade a marauding dragon to voluntarily throw itself into the sea, and I suppose that's a transferable skill of sorts.

This earth-covered refuge at Lanrivoaré evokes the contrast in Saint Hervé's own life, between the simple existence of a hermit and the prestige he enjoyed in the wider religious context of western Brittany. We saw in Chapter 2 how important his presence was felt to be at the excommunication of Conomor. Nothing could be further from a crowd of speechifying people and political manipulations than the calm beauty of this special grove. Such notions perhaps symbolise a deeper disparity, the difference between what is sometimes called 'Celtic Christianity' and the more formalised Church of Rome which was well-established elsewhere in Brittany. The religion of hermits settled in such an environment as this was close to nature on its own terms rather than an exertion of power over it. The idea that there could be worship in such a place is redolent of paganism.

If chapels are themselves in essence a protective cover for worship, what can be said of the extraordinary setting of another former hermitage, once of natural origins but later transformed into what today is one of the most famous sights in Brittany. The **troglodyte chapel of St Gildas** is wedged into a huge overhang of granite on the banks of the Blavet in the commune of Bieuzy, like a victim trapped in the stone mouth of a monster. According to the legend, the saint arrived with his follower Bieuzy in this idyllic spot in 537 and they made the most of a natural recess in the rock to create a shelter for spiritual retreat, away from the demands of monastery life at the Abbaye Saint-Gildas-du-Rhys. But when word of the illustrious saint's presence spread, many came to hear the wisdom of Gildas and he preached from the steps outside his retreat. He is said to have summoned followers to a session by using the ringing stone, outside in those days but now housed in the chapel, perched on a granite pillar. This special stone is to be stroked in a circle with a smaller one to emit a metallically musical noise. One can't help thinking a good old bell would have been rather more effective. (For more on ringing stones, see p.178.) Visitors now may have to run the gauntlet of an ostentation of local peacocks, which like to intimidate interlopers and hang around determinedly for picnic fare. They make quite a sight spread over the steps in front of the chapel, as if waiting for a sermon.

The original cavity in the rock was turned into two oratories to accommodate the two saints. It was not until the 15th century that a proper chapel was constructed. This was heavily remodelled in the 19th, with a second part added in 1837 on the western end, giving the semi-detached appearance it has today. The actual spot on the shores of the Blavet retains some of that idyllic atmosphere that attracted the two saints in the first place. Nearby the river flows below Castennec, the rocky high point where the enigmatic Venus de Quinipily (see p.115) once stood.

Monks from his monastery eventually came to take Gildas back to his duties, but Bieuzy remained, concentrating on creating a school and providing Christian education for all those in the area. Unusually though for one of the Breton saints, he came to a sad end. The local lord sent a servant to summon the saint to cure his pack of hunting hounds, all suffering from rabies. Bieuzy was celebrating mass and refused to break off the service. The nobleman was so furious at this slight that he arrived with an axe and from behind brought it down with all his force into the holy man's head. It remained there, stuck, whilst Bieuzy finished the divine offices and then made the eighty kilometre journey on foot in order to die with his mentor Gildas at Saint-Gildas-du-Rhys. The perpetrator of this terrible crime was eaten by his own raging animals. Not surprisingly, Bieuzy was subsequently invoked for headaches, on the grounds of expert witness, and was also a sure thing for granting protection from rabies.

From physical protection to spiritual sanctuary, from burial to primitive dwelling, the notion of cover and the focused energy of enclosed spaces has given rise to many stories, but imaginative power can also be harnessed to draw us closer to the original inhabitants and constructors of these sites, who felt the darkness of peace and finality they embody.

4 Elevation

As cover separates and protects from the above, other structures rise into the sky, demanding attention and invading the element of air. The human instinct to achieve this height in architecture surely goes all the way back to early man standing on two feet for better defensive visibility. The urge developed quite new motivations as understanding of the potential of stone began. A challenge to surpass human scale was launched. Standing-stones, church spires, lighthouses are all around in Brittany, upright thrusts flaunting themselves for everyone to heed, spikes of energy of one sort or another, faith or science based or both. In legend and reality they encapsulate stories of man's aspiration, designed to impress as well as to use altitude for practical purpose, or to provide solid expression of reverence.

This architecture of up marks the landscape in a special way, providing focal points for travellers on land and sea, revealing settlement and the boundaries of human control, expressing both warning of danger and the reassurance of familiar sights. Stone is solid against the invisibility of air, but air holds the definition of upright structures, shaping the space of their context. Raised stone weathers and breaks over time in the playground of the winds, and many a menhir and religious monument has been diminished through storm activity. While standing-stones are often associated with fertility, thanks to their sometimes very phallic appearance, the sexual connotation of the vertical erection can hardly be applied to church steeples, where the trajectory is towards the glory of God. Neither can compete in measurement with modern high-points, transmitters of one sort or another reaching 300m up into the sky, but their impact on the landscape remains immensely powerful and often exuberant. They draw our vision from afar.

Out in the far west beyond Brest are the huge standing-stones, the highest in Brittany and in France. They have an affinity of material, the pinkish granite of Aber Ildut, and of habit: all go off to drink in the ocean on the first stroke of midnight on Christmas night, leaving the treasure they guard exposed. But they are back before the sound of the bells dies away, and woe betide anyone foolish enough to make an attempt on the gold in that short time… Tales of moving menhirs are part of the magic of the Breton landscape in folklore, the vivid sense of a layer of life beyond what the eye can easily see. There is also the notion of them behaving like humans, a hint of the theory that some represent actual people or a symbolic ancestor. This particular story of assuaging thirst is commonly told of standing-stones elsewhere too, but there is something singular and memorable about these probably once aligned individuals.

Four kilometres from the ancient capital of Saint-Renan, the **Menhir de Kerloas** is undisputed king, 'a superb needle of granite' according to our friend the Chevalier de Freminville, standing at an astonishing 9.5m. It would have been higher still had it not lost its top in an 18th century storm, with one of the resulting fragments used for a field boundary stone and another made into a trough. Perhaps as much as 2m of root is buried in the earth, with the circumference at base measuring 6.2m, increasing to 6.96m before finally tapering away into the distinctive sloping peak. About a metre above the ground the stone has two small shaped protuberances on opposite sides, which have been the major factor in its reputation for powerful fertility rites. Weathering has obscured (possibly original) engravings on the face of the menhir, but seven cup-marks can still be seen and, in a very good light only, the lines of two crosses. According to an early illustration, it was once marked by a cross on the top, but this is now gone.

Menhir de Kerloas

The menhir is set at an altitude of 132m, a few metres lower than the summit of the highest rise in this part of the historical region of Léon (northern Finistère). The nearest source material was 2km away and would have necessitated an uphill drag, impressive feat in itself with such a colossal weight. Although we can't be sure of its exact relation to the many other standing-stones in the area, it seems foolhardy to dismiss correlation of some kind. The stone is visible from up to 30km away, as far as the higher parts of the modern city of Brest, and would have been a significant navigational aid. If it is drawing attention to a particular spot, advertising a grave, for example, as some have claimed, there could hardly be better publicity than this massive column.

Whilst it has attracted generic folklore, such as concealing buried treasure and having the capacity for movement, Kerloas has long been best known as the scene of fertility rites, drawing on the phallic appearance of the stone. Stories of its 'success' would have been spread by word of mouth, entering the local tradition of stones with power. Married couples were urged to rub their stomachs against the two protuberances near the foot of the column. One version said this would ensure male children for the husband, another that the woman's motivation was to win control of the household afterwards. A waspish analysis makes these the two fundamental aspirations of Breton peasants. An alternative method was for the man and woman each to kiss one side of the menhir. If their lips were parallel, they would have only male children. These days ritual seems to continue in the general spirit of procreation, going by the pairs of knickers left fluttering along the hedgerows from time to time. In the early 20th century, historian Georges Guénin wrote that the menhir was thought to have general healing powers, and people came in the hope of cures for any illnesses by rubbing themselves on the bosses. Certainly such an astonishingly large and commanding stone emits a sense of potency whatever one's needs or desires, hence creating a place for expressing wishes of all kinds.

In 1832 that ubiquitous Chevalier de Freminville believed it part of the Celtic religion, like the generally earlier dolmens, suggesting that this particular standing-stone marked the burial place of an important chieftain, interpreting the name Ker-loas as 'place of grief'. A veritable tale was worked up from this, with a newspaper article of October 1833 repeating the idea, citing examples of human remains dug up near various menhirs, and says that some famous or self-important person wanted to really stand out from the crowd even in death, so his name would not be lost. (In which case, failure, as only the stone has an identity today.) The author speculates that the chief must have been prescient about the rise of Brest as the region's capital (displacing Saint-Renan) and becoming an important international maritime city, and selected his burial site out of a determination to be visible to its inhabitants. How's that for funeral planning?

The article goes on to speculate boldly on the identity of the buried man and make the daringly optimistic connection with a nearby château, which apparently had an oddly ancient appearance, that perhaps long ago was the home of the chief. It ends with the funny story of three men seeking treasure at the foot of the menhir. This common theme of folklore has real historical significance. It was a common peasant belief that nobles fleeing the territory in the Dark Ages had buried their valuables under the tall stones, which may seem rather obvious aide-memoires. There is an important general truth here about burials elsewhere, as archaeology has shown, and this genuine connection with stories of buried riches should not be forgotten – let's think coin hoards rather than elf-gold. So the men started to dig but heard strange noises and suddenly two devils appeared, with claws, pointed tails, diamonds for eyes, and glowing coals in their mouths. They fell to the ground in fearful stupor and did not come round until the cock crowed and the light of dawn spread over the scene. In place of evil spirits, there were only two local farmers who had come to see who was on their land trying to steal from the menhir...

We may not be able to say with any certainty what the menhirs were for originally, but the overwhelming achievement of raising enormous stones skywards – and often stones moved over considerable distances – must have been a statement intended to inspire stunned admiration. We often focus on our own reactions of awe and wonder today: would contemporary assessment have been any different? The mastery of processes involved in extracting, shaping, transporting and erecting were a skill-set that must surely have raised the status of those involved in achieving such an end result. And what gods could fail to look kindly on the creators of these majestic columns? Alignments only multiply the sense of amazement commonly felt in their presence. There may have been an element of competition involved too, an instinct for community pride in these first enduring monuments of mankind in neolithic times, revelling in the element of stone that was to be the arbiter of their achievement. (The same vying to outdo other groups would be a factor nearly 5000 years later in building the spires of the parish closes. See p.77.) Reaching upwards for the sheer sense of what was newly possible, perhaps expressing reverence for sky power and tracing cosmological patterns.

The height of standing-stones makes us think of them often as markers and signposts, but for what? If generally they date to the later neolithic years, what is their relation with the earlier monuments? Perhaps the uprights marked burial sites and cemeteries, or ceremonial spaces. Perhaps in conjunction they laid down a matrix of posts pointing out important lines of travel and communication, connecting places of habitation or seasonal celebration, like 3D maps. Those within sight of the coast were presumably intended to help sea voyagers, just as menhirs continued to serve as important day-marks later on. The location and placing of each standing-stone will have depended on one or several of these *raisons d'etre*, and yet their unfathomable practicality continues to yield mystery, which fortunately usually leads to anecdotal appropriation...

Eight kilometres from Kerloas is **Kergadiou**. If there were no trees to block the line of sight, these two great standing-stones would be able to greet each other directly. This one is a heart-stoppingly imposing monument, 8.75m tall, set on the high plain in a clearer context than Kerloas, standing slim, straight and strong, the Clint Eastwood of Breton menhirs. Situated on a shoulder of land, a dozen metres below the apex, this special stone is also widely visible, and there is a mysterious and intangible sense of the sea not far away. Here the land is more open and this intensifies the impact of both stones, because the upright has a mate lying sixty metres away, at an angle of 18° to the ground, another fine stone with a wide, well-worked flat side uppermost, tilted upwards like a ramp or runway, ready for launch. It is over 9m long, but opinion is divided on whether it was ever raised, although the labour invested would suggest that was the idea. An unseen thread of connection sparks between the two stones like the result of a long marriage.

The two date from c3000BC, with Bronze and Iron Age artefacts found in the vicinity. Both are from the characteristic porphyroid granite of the area with its striking pink feldspath, the upright stone worked assiduously to give the smooth sides and streamlined shape that impress by their simple clarity. Their carefully chosen location must have been a focal point in the landscape, a landmark for navigation, a link in the sequence of stone signals across the highland of the interior, an area that was to figure largely in the later tin route that centred on Saint-Renan. The important height is reflected in the fact that the Germans put a viewing platform on the top of the Kergadiou stone during the Occupation of WWII, as apparently one could see as far as the English coasts in good weather. That's an extraordinary visual of combined ancient and modern prowess.

There is something pure and self-contained about this giant and it does not seem to have attracted the fertility legends of Kerloas. The story recorded by M. Taburet in 1925 is odder: a woman (probably a fairy given her power) stole the standing-stone from a witch in Great Britain and brought it to Armorica in her silk apron. The witch was furious and screamed that crime would not pay and she would break the menhir. She threw another huge stone in her fury towards Kergadiou but it fell onto the ground where it lies now. The tale interestingly may reflect less than happy exchanges between England and Brittany during the naval conflicts of the 18th and 19th centuries, or even earlier, but here the stone, without the back-story of why it might have been snatched in the first place, other than making a cracking souvenir, seems unfortunately in the negative category of 'stolen goods'. The vibe is confusing, but this one doesn't need a legend. It's good enough to stand alone.

Another of the fine menhirs in this coastal area is that of **Kerhouezel**, once called the **Menhir de Kereneur**. It stands 6.6m high at an altitude of 37m and sports an orange tip, presumably from weathered lichen, giving the stone a rusty appearance. The familiar pink flecked granite from up the road glistens in the summer sunshine, which also marks the faint silvery line round a natural hedgehog-shaped shallow protuberance towards the top. The setting of the menhir is much more enclosed, with field boundaries close by and houses visible at hand, so there is not the same sense of height driving up into space as the others, but certainly the same solidity of presence and the same impression of calm permanence. Crops permitting, it is possible to force a way through a hedge and cross to the stone itself. When Georges Guénin was collecting information about local stones in the 1930s, he was assured by a fisherman from Lanildut that this menhir could turn itself round – a singular feat – and even went to swim in the sea from time to time. One can almost believe it.

The menhirs now are far from being the only celestial furniture, with the considerably higher practical giants of pylons, wind-farms, antennae and water-towers competing even with ubiquitous church spires for air space and the prize of visibility. Modern technology has rendered all these many times taller than neolithic monuments (which we should remember had no other architecture to emulate), but they still earn their place in this network of elevated structures. For those who see standing-stones as energy sources, accessing deep-held resources inside the earth, like stone needles in an act of telluric acupuncture, there is an even closer connection with modern vehicles of power. Researchers draw grids and angles to show a complex network of the many monuments in this area, but above all else it seems to me that these large menhirs primarily draw attention to the sky, a medium of contrast in density and fluidity. Reaching up so far beyond the scale of humans is, at the very least, pure aspiration, expressing the ambition of a community.

Church spires form a similar web of connection to that of the menhirs (including all those now lost), stretching out a chain of settlements through the landscape. They too mark location, give direction and provide an impressive attestation of faith. The bell-tower below was also of great significance in marking the time of services and providing the villagers with a soundtrack to all major events of life. These vertical statements reach up towards heaven pointing to the glory of God, echoing the high cross on many calvaries, which were a reminder of the ascension of Christ. The achievement of medieval builders is as great, relatively speaking, as that of the people who erected the neolithic standing-stones. There is enormous variation of style and decoration, reflecting the development of architecture from Romanesque tower-style to the iconic Flamboyant Gothic so beloved in Brittany, later Renaissance refinements and the solid worthies of the late 19th century.

It is also interesting to note adaptations to the landscape, as strikingly shown in the case of **Commana** and **Plouneour-Menez**. These two churches stand just to the north of the Monts d'Arrée, exposed to the harsh weather conditions that sweep across the moors and rocky peaks. The terrain is rude and wild, the wind a serious player in conditions of survival. The identical spires of the two churches are reflective of this: dour and forbidding with none of the delicate lightness achieved in contemporary stone in less exposed circumstances. They cannot risk the lightening of their weight created by many openings in the structure, and so rise up much like the schist summits looming over them, stoic, solid and remarkably durable. These are both examples of **parish closes** (*enclos paroissiaux*), an ensemble of religious architecture for which the region of Léon is famous, and which reflects the prosperity generated by the cloth trade with England. The *enclos* consists of a walled precinct, usually with monumental entrance, containing the church, a calvary, and an ossuary or charnel house. Even small villages may boast one of these remarkably elaborate (and expensive) hymns in stone, the sort of public expression of communal faith that was more valued than individual ostentation in western Brittany. But local pride meant not only ambition to commission the best craftsmen, but also a resolution to outdo neighbouring efforts. Rivalry was at the root of the towering height of many churches. **Lampaul-Guimiliau**, very close to the exquisite *enclos* at **Guimiliau**, was determined to dominate the skyline with its enormous bell-tower (1573) reaching a dizzying 75m before the lightning strike of 1809 that reduced it by 18m. It has never been restored due to the equally soaring cost, and remains in its truncated state, still a sizeable landmark and point of orientation around the outskirts of Landivisiau.

There are also some wonderful oddities in this world of church uprights. Perhaps the most notable of all is not famous for its

Église Lampaul-Guimiliau

height. The **Chapelle Saint Gonéry** at Plougrescant in northern Côtes d'Armor with its crooked witch's hat of a spire, is certainly memorable, but rather failing in its premier purpose of surging upwards. The original building is a 12th century Romanesque oratory, which may also have served as a fire-tower (see below), with the chapel later expanded in Gothic style. The spire was added in 1612, with the unfortunate choice of lead as material. The base with its ancient timbers, proved too weak to support this heavy metal steeple, and each began to lean in different directions. It looks like something from a fairy-tale now, but the explanation is disappointingly prosaic and no miracles involved, except perhaps that it didn't fall over soon after construction. Work to secure the tower once and for all was started in 1962, but the inhabitants were adamant that they didn't want it straightened!

The chapel contains the tomb and relic of the skull of Saint Gon(n)ery. This saint was from Ireland, arriving in Brittany in the 6th century, and initially settling as a hermit in the Forêt de Branguily near Rohan. Here Gonery incurred the wrath of the lord by not noticing him, so absorbed was the saint in his prayers. The nobleman's servants beat him up and left him for dead, but were soon struck by paralysis and afflictions themselves. A miracle by the restored saint released them, after abject apologies from their master, who then converted to Christianity. This is a conventional enough story used of other Breton saints, but a unique, as far as I know, tale is told of Gonery's subsequent career. He was asked to perform a wedding, and converted some stones (probably a dolmen) into a chapel for the service. This seems a bizarre notion in itself, if it was not done with particular intent of appropriation. During the ceremony, an evil spirit broke off a large rock, hoping to crush all those below, but the saint gestured with his hand, like a magician, and the stone stopped in mid-air, allowing the marriage to be completed. What happened then isn't recorded... The purpose of the story is to show another miracle, of course, but here it is the power over nature (and the laws of physics). If the 'evil spirit' was in some way a guardian of the pagan site, resenting the forced conversion of the rocks to Christianity, then it is another sort of triumph, over an object of heathen worship. And a more interesting story.

The spire of the **Kreisker chapel** in Saint-Pol-de-Léon can be seen from far and wide, easily winning the height contest with the nearby cathedral spires. It is traditionally the highest in Brittany at 78m, a Gothic granite wonder. (Admittedly there is a bit of a recent dispute here with Saint-Martin de Vertou in Ille-et-Vilaine.) Four miniature bell-towers surround the base above the cornice, and the octagonal form is decorated with numerous flower-shaped (rosette) openings, giving the slender structure its lacy appearance. Vauban, Louis XIV's architect, regarded it as the boldest architectural work he had ever seen. Popular belief of the time held it so splendid that it was claimed an angel descending from the sky to earth would choose to first place his foot on top of this spire. Today the chapel houses an altar of the *Tro Breiz*, the pilgrimage around the seven cathedrals of Brittany, with mini-statues of the seven founding saints, including the patron of the town and its cathedral, Saint Pol. The name Kreisker means 'the town centre' whereas the chapel was actually in the line of fortifications surrounding the heart of the settlement, at the lower end of the main street from the cathedral.

The founding story of the chapel is one of punishment and redemption, although it may sit uneasily with modern values. On a feast day of the Virgin Mary, Saint Guévroc (Guirec) was passing through on his way to the cathedral when he saw a young woman still at home, toiling away at laundry. He reprimanded her for working on this religious holiday, but she refused to heed him, saying that she must do so to survive, and take any opportunity to make a living. No sooner had she said this than her limbs became paralysed and she could not move her hands or feet. She remained in this state for days, constantly praying for release, and finally was carried by neighbours into the presence of the saint. She begged for forgiveness and uttered solemn repentance for her insult to the Virgin. Guévroc made the sign of the cross to release her from her torment and restored movement in her body. As a grand gesture of remorse, she willed her house to the Church to be consecrated as a chapel to the Virgin Mary. The legend, recorded by Albert Le Grand (b.c1599), a Dominican monk from Morlaix, does not comment on the unusual situation of a young woman living alone in the first place, without relatives to object to such a lavish gift of property.

The early form of the chapel was burnt in Viking raids of the 9th century. Rebuilt in stone, it was burnt again, this time by the English in an attack on 3rd May 1375. The campaign was part of the Wars of Succession that raged all over Brittany with one side supported by the French king Charles V and the other by Edward III of England. Once again the chapel was rebuilt soon after and it is thought that the English garrison in Saint-Pol must have had a hand in the new construction. There are elements that certainly seem to come from the Perpendicular style at the base of the tower, but the motives of the English were unlikely to have been religious: a move to adapt the tower into a well-placed look-out station over the Channel makes more sense. Its proximity to the coast accounts for the long, thin arched open windows which can mitigate the effects of winds off the sea. The bell-tower, accessed by a narrow staircase, gained its famous spire between 1439 and 1472. The style derived from the Norman influence of the church of Saint-Pierre in Caen (1317) and Notre-Dame du Mur (total elevation 85m) in nearby Morlaix. It survived several lightning strikes in the next two hundred years, and proved itself a real survivor when more serious existential threat arose.

Saint-Pol-de-Léon suffered a tragic fate at the time of the Revolution. The bishopric was suppressed, as each new department was to have only one, and Quimper as capital of Finistère took the prize. This brought a period of decline to this once prosperous and strong commercial town. The Kreisker chapel fell into ruin and parts were demolished for the stone. Moves to destroy the tower, however, met with local opposition as it enjoyed a special place in the hearts of the population. People rallied to save their spire and finally an appeal to the highest power in the land was not only made, but successful. Napoleon himself signed a decree in 1807 to spare the bell-tower on the grounds of its significance as a navigational aid, and France needed all the help it could get on that front as imperial wars fomented. The survival of the Kreisker spire contrasted with the sad fate of its rival Notre-Dame du Mur twenty kilometres down the road, which fell down in 1806 after the post-Revolutionary owner began carting away the stone beneath it for building projects!

It is not only church spires that illustrate the importance of elevation in faith. The ubiquitous calvaries, from simple wayside crosses to complex multi-layered monuments like the *enclos* at Saint-Thégonnec or Guéhenno, express the same sentiments with more specific focus. These latter stone structures were in effect teaching aids, used by the priests in educating their often illiterate flocks about the Passion of Christ, the events of his last days and what happened after the crucifixion. Money was lavished on the finest sculptures or the greatest number of figures. Standing on the way in and out of the church porch as constant reminders, they tell the crucial story of death and resurrection, with Jesus himself often shown on the upper level with a finger pointing directly upwards towards his heavenly destination. Even the exquisite talents of the 17th century stone-carvers who crafted these monuments couldn't find a more dramatic representation of ascension, although the friezes of events of Holy Week on *calvaires* are certainly precursors of the comic strip narrative. But the message is clear: the goal of the Christian is to go up not down. Sometimes this is made painfully explicit with a depiction of the mouth of Hell, shown as that of a great monster, as a reminder of the alternative. At Guimiliau, where the calvary has more than 200 figures, Katel Gollet, a young woman who (allegedly) preferred drinking and dancing to fulfilling the demands of faith, is shown naked (her bare breasts rather fondly portrayed), being dragged by demons down into the torturous depths of the inferno. Up is an even more striking dimension when the opposite is given form.

ELEVATION

For something unusual beyond the crowded field of more traditional calvaries, it is worth a look at one in **Trégastel** (Côtes d'Armor). This strikingly elevated monument on the Butte de Crec'h Lest was erected in 1872 at the highest point in the commune. To say it is a stone mound with a cross on top is hardly to do justice to the lofty height or the sheer peculiarity of this relatively modern *calvaire*. It was constructed through the determination of Abbé Jean-Jacques Bourget, who suffered a humiliating audience at Versailles with the Catholic deputies as he tried to raise money for the project. They were not impressed by this Breton-speaking farmer's son from Lower Brittany and scorned the proposal. He came away from a brief meeting with the President of the Republic with nothing more than a patronising 10

Le Calvaire de Trégastel

franc coin contribution. When news of this cruel rejection spread locally around Trégastel, funds began to pour in for the new construction, which became a kind of community project to unite the parishioners, who donated their money and their labour.

They worked to create this rough dry-stone structure with vague echoes of dolmens in the curious stone arches on the incline, and of grottoes with a crypt-like chapel of Notre-Dame de la Pitié underpinning the entire structure. The calvary was also a direct tool of evangelisation, with religious exhortations in Breton, and statues of Catholic worthies in niches up the narrow spiral external pathway providing an upward 'journey'. There is no barrier on this precarious route and this is a rare occasion when one almost wishes for a bit of imposed health and safety, but the 360° view is a reward. Even at this very modest height, there is a real sense of escaping from the surface of earth to a higher plane. The air may not be more rarefied, but the idea of spiritual progression is clearly factored in, reminding us that up is the way to go.

At the start is a Breton peasant kneeling, hat in hand, and spade at the ready – the quotation states the value of this simple, sincere and practical faith against those whose airy abstractions and mere words are of little effect. A smack in the face for Versailles there? On the north-facing platform, François Xavier, a Basque saint, waves his fist in the air. Above that is a solid stone stack of considerable height in proportion to the rest, beautifully made and mortared, reflecting a later more financially secure stage of building. This is topped by an enormous cross, a replacement for the one destroyed by lightning in 1912. Even admirable pious projects like this, evidence of the strong commitment of faith, ultimately can't compete with the power of air. The vulnerability of elevated monuments of all kinds and the open target of pinnacles becomes all too apparent under the pressure of violent storms.

Perhaps most threatened of all by extreme weather are the sentinels of the Breton shores. The lighthouse has become an iconic symbol of Brittany, a land surrounded on three sides by sea, key to the Channel entrance and with a maritime history second to none. These beacons, so prevalent along Brittany's coast, explore the relation between sea and sky in architectural form and function, often appearing to fuse with the rocks on which they are built. They are the epitome of determination rather than aspiration, representing the astonishing feat of construction in that totally inauspicious place – the moving ocean. Like the standing-stones, they are guardians, providing warning points and directional information. The sheer relief of seeing their light shine out in dark stormy nights must be incalculable to those on the sea. The achievement of elevation in such unimaginably difficult conditions is a story in itself, but the resistance and endurance of stone has been crucial to the survival of these marine menhirs, most notably in the turbulent waters of the Atlantic.

The earliest form were terrestrial fire towers, such as that surviving in about two thirds of its original at the **Abbaye Saint-Mathieu** on almost the westernmost point of France. Traditionally this was founded in the 6th century by Saint Tanguy to expiate his guilt after murdering his sister Haude. He believed the lies of their wicked step-mother, and beheaded poor Haude before hearing her side of the story (of inchastity). The relics of the Apostle Matthew were brought back from Egypt by Breton sailors. Legend says that on their arrival at this shore a massive rock blocking the path of the boat dramatically split into two parts to allow their passage, which was why this site was decided on for the 12th century version of the abbey. The dramatic cliff-top location now has a 'modern' lighthouse (1830) slotted into the ruins of the ancient monastery, which include the *tour à feu*. Here the monks kept a torch in an enclosed lantern structure as a hazard warning for ships of the royal navy in the area at night, a service mentioned in a text of 1681. Seventy years later, the lantern was ripped off by a stormy gust of wind.

Further south on this dangerous Atlantic coast is the **Phare de Tévennec** (1869), a lighthouse perched on a lonely rock, guarding the tempestuous Raz de Sein between the culmination of Cap Sizun in the Pointe du Raz and the low Île de Sein a little over five kilometres out to sea. A lighthouse said to be cursed and haunted. It was constructed soon after the Phare Ar Men, one of the most perilously situated of all, and the Phare de la Vieille, the little lighthouse nearby, followed in 1879 to provide a triangle of protection. I can attest to the capricious and potentially vicious nature of the strait. This is the only stretch of water where I've suffered seasickness, on my first visit to the tiny island of Sein many years ago. Traditionally lighthouse guardians categorise their locations as Paradise, Purgatory or Hell, according to whether they are placed on shore/in an estuary, or on an island which is less accessible, or in full sea, totally cut off for the vast majority of the time, like Ar Men. Tévennec was technically a purgatory post, but it was to prove hell for many of its keepers.

The rock of Tévennec appears high in calm seas but it is soon subsumed in foaming waves as the waters mount. On a first glance the lighthouse looks in profile decidedly like a chapel, an image only intensified by the strange sight of a cross placed on the rocks on the edge of the enclosure around the structure, which consists of the tower and the keeper's accommodation. There is nothing else. Nothing grows here and it's almost impossible to get a boat in. When the lighthouse was manned, supplies could only be delivered once a fortnight, if that. Life there was dispiriting, isolated and ultimately wretched for many who tried and failed to cope with the challenge. There is something singular in its situation and no surprise that this place has acquired a fearsome reputation as a haunted habitat, a story perhaps beginning with the reality of a shipwrecked sailor washed up but quite unable to be saved, suffering a lingering death over five long days. He was only one of a much greater number of bodies that have found their way to this forsaken rock.

Work began on the lighthouse in 1869 at the same time as that of Ar Men, much further out in the ocean, so labourers could double up on these arduous projects according to the state of sea and sky. Men claimed even at that early stage to have seen apparitions and heard harrowing cries, doubtless the spirits of the dead accumulated in this unlucky place. The light shone out for the first time in March 1875.

The first keeper, Henri Guézennec, was soon established in his lonely post. He was to last less than three years, driven mad by the endless eerie sounds echoing around the rock. They seemed to him to call relentlessly in Breton '*Kers cuit, kers cuit, Ama ma ma flag!*' (Go away, Go away, This is my place). He could not bear to continue on the rock. Alain Menou arrived to replace him but the same story of mental torment ensued. So bad a reputation did the lighthouse now have that a priest from Cap Sizun was called out to bless the rock and a cross was mounted to emphasise that God was watching over those marooned in this desolate place. In recent times divers discovered a tunnel under the rock which probably accounted for the strangely echoing noises interpreted as supernatural cries by forlorn men stranded in the middle of a churning bowl of surging waves.

But ill-fortune seemed wedded to those walls, inbuilt with the overwhelming humidity that weighed down and trapped the spirits of dead and living alike. Even a dispensation for occasional help from the guardian of La Vieille to relieve the constant intensity of the burdensome post made no difference. The sorry saga continued, few applied for the position and few stayed. There were three deaths and a bizarre accident with a knife that caused serious injury… The authorisation in 1897 for the keeper to be accompanied by his wife did not seem to change the fortunes of Tévennec. There was one exception, however: between 1900 and 1905 the Quémere family established themselves, together with chickens, a pig and a cow. And a young child. To which three more were added during their tenure, which suggests a success of sorts. At least their experience provides something of a balance to the dire tales of fated disasters. But eventually they transferred to another post. The next guardian died of a heart-attack and his wife had to use salt to try to preserve the body until relief arrived. A child died when part of the roof fell in during a storm. This was not an auspicious place.

The family Ropars were the last occupants, but the keeper and his wife were unable to resist the history of ill-fortune they faced. Ropars' father-in-law was swept away by a wave during a visit, and his wife suffered a complicated birth with the infant dying soon after. Their departure was the end of the line for the lighthouse's human occupants. In 1910 an automatic light was established and no more keepers struggled for health and sanity in the confined quarters on the cursed rock. This fire in the sky designed to save lives at sea was in fact for the men and woman courageous enough to take on such a testing experience, a story of tragedy.

Raising tall structures like all of these is to create something outside the norm, to push man's abilities to literal high points. Up feels like a celebration in this context, just as down and darkness can mean sadness or grief. The triumph of survival is also there in the menhirs, astonishing legacy of still relatively unknown people from the far past, the church architecture going strong in times of considerable upheaval of beliefs, and those stalwart lighthouses grimly clinging on to their foundations, still alive with unmanned light at the peak, like a tree growing out of a rock. It's right we should continue to salute them, relevant to human scale as they are, and all the upward trending heritage they represent in contrast with sleek modern towers, reaching ever more remotely into the skies.

5 Stone boats

It is well known that the Breton saints (who in a strict sense were neither Bretons nor saints) arrived from Britain onto Armorican shores in stone boats. This detail is an essential part of many advent tales from the oral tradition and certain hagiographies. The bare 'fact' was intended to shout MIRACLE, for everyone knows stones don't float. Except, of course, they do.

In 2002 a granite vessel, the **Maen Vag** (stone boat) was constructed by Jean-Yves Menez to indicate the potential veracity of these extraordinary stories that seem to defy natural laws. But any craft conforming to the laws of physics – displacing a volume of water superior in weight to the craft's own weight – will remain buoyant. His sleek construction floats well and has made various journeys with crew. So the idea of a stone boat holds water. But it rather undermines that old miracle angle, quite apart from being totally impractical.

The theme of the stone boats is in line with a traditional motif of magical crossings, deriving ultimately in the Christian story from Moses passing over the Red Sea dry-footed and Jesus walking on water. The particularly Breton version of lithic Channel crossings is a reflection of the exceptional coastline of the Armorican peninsula where a vast shoreline is littered with rocks of all shapes and sizes. Looks like a boat, found on a beach, chances are it's a stone vessel, just as monster shaped rocks have inspired tales of ravaging beasts. And who could manage to sail that unheard of thing, a stone boat – why, a saint of course! The boat-like stones were imaginative props to the miraculous arrival of the holy men and women, an element of local identity, and a confirmation of the saints' role in the foundation of early Breton society, before Brittany as such existed.

In terms of a story thread, the stone boat comes somewhere between biblical tales and later feats of healing attributed to the stones themselves. But the elemental relationship between stone and water goes back considerably further to the megalithic construction of the neolithic world, and the probable significance of sources and rivers in the placing of many monuments from that time (see Chapter 6). The stone boats saga presents another layer of the Christian determination to take power over the elements, here the special dynamism of earth and water, and prove their god superior to the forces of nature which are at the heart of paganism. The journeys of the saints must have been even more impressive to an audience well aware of the ever-present dangers of travel over water and exposure to storms at sea. The symbolism of the stone boat was an important factor in the legendary world of these wonder-workers, so seminal in the origins of Brittany itself.

So sticking with the Christian version, in days long before scientific analysis, the Channel crossing in stone boats was a miraculous act. It demonstrated the exceptional power of these holy men who represented the new religion. What a splash to make on turning up atop a slab of stone! How literally awesome! Imagine a bunch of Breton fisherman in their scruffy little wicker craft seeing Saint Ronan dodge in and out of their path as he skimmed the waves of the Bay of Douarnenez on his lump of granite. (It was an arresting start that he failed to capitalise on, having to move inland sharpish after accusing the coastal folk of being sinful wreckers.) Saint Tudy crossed to the Île de Groix on a menhir. Saint Vougay in Ireland commanded a great rock on the shore to break off and carry him wherever God willed. It took him to the coast of Brittany at Penmarc'h before he moved on to Léon where his eponymous village can be found today. But these rocky relics were to go on to provide the physical 'evidence' for foundation legends, as well as for the saints' dazzling thaumaturgy.

So far, so obvious. Many rocks are decidedly boat-shaped, with a worn dip in the middle and higher sides. But it can't be as simple as that: some 'stone boats' are to be found in considerably more inland positions and require a suitably adapted explanation. The **Bateau de Saint Conogan** lies 500m from the Pointe du Millier with its lighthouse, in the shady valley of the Moulin de Keriolet. One end rests on a flat rock, with the prow, or maybe stern, raised into the air. To incorporate this location, the story is that it struck a rock on the beach at Porz Peron and flew through the air to its current emplacement. The saint must have been seriously speeding. It is probably a dislodged menhir or a lying stone that was never actually erected, but its impressive measurements at 8m in length and slightly curved shape lend it a tale of its own and a naval history. Other stone boats found far from the beach are said to have been moved by human (or animal) force to honour locations dedicated to the relevant saint.

Saint Conogan's stone boat

There's no shortage of surviving stories or actual stones here. There is also no shortage of more prosaic explanations. Stones may have been carried to sea by normal craft, which were constructed using wood, reeds or skins, to stabilise the mast or to set a fire safely for cooking, but they were also used for onboard ballast, that could be jettisoned at need. The tales of stone boats appearing in written accounts, such as those of Albert Le Grand in the 17th century, may have sprung from such medieval remains in evidence on the Breton shoreline. Like what happened to the craft carrying Saint Pol from Ouessant to the mainland of Brittany under duress from a tempest. Some said it was actually his prayer stone and the crew were fed up with the kneeling saint cluttering up the deck. Another version has the ballast thrown overboard in response to the stormy conditions. Whether they took severe action or whether the boat was wrecked and he was a miraculous survivor saved by his floating stone acting as a life-raft, Pol is said to have arrived on the northern coast near where the little lighthouse of Pontsuval stands now, complete with this heavy accompaniment. It was later dragged inland towards the settlement to honour the saint. The poor horse tasked with that job gave up the struggle on the nearest knoll, where today the stone remains in a little chapel dedicated to Saint Pol.

Saint Seny or Sezny arrived from Ireland on the north shore of Brittany near Kerlouan in a stone *auge* or trough. He wanted to establish a church but another saint was there before him, so he threw a stone (or a hammer) as far as he could. This turned out to be two kilometres, where it fell into a field of flax which next day was miraculously ready for cultivation. This was where he created his settlement, today known as the village of Guisseny. In *Les derniers Bretons* Emile Souvestre records a story he was told on the spot by a peasant – that Seny built his first chapel in a single night as all the stones turned up of their own accord and placed themselves carefully in the structure 'like sheep returning to the fold'. Another tale said God intended to make Seny patron of women but he was horrified and begged to be given tailors or ropemakers instead. 'If you are so delicate as that,' God replied, 'I'll give you an even greater task. You will become the patron of sick dogs.' Seny was overjoyed at this reprieve. I suspect this shows the peasant's sense of humour rather than God's. The stone boat apparently became a sarcophagus for the saint on his death.

There's another possibility. What if some medieval scribe simply muddled the words *cumba* (Latin for little boat) with the Old Breton *koum* (a valley or by its shape, a trough)? A 17th century wooden altarpiece on the wall in the church at Porspoder shows scenes from the life of Saint Budoc, including his arrival from Cornwall. Here his vessel is a rectangular stone basin of the kind one might happily plant up after watching Gardeners' World. The same can be seen in Yann d'Argent's well-known painting of Saint Houardon in his chapel at Landerneau, pushed across the waters by two angels on his stone trough. It's not beyond belief that such a small linguistic error started the trend. We have only to think of Saint Tudwal or Tudgual, one of the seven founding saints of Brittany, now known as Tugdual after a transposition error in copying.

But the crossing was not the end of the story. The stones themselves, imbued with power by saintly progress, often took on a life of their own further down the line. They were said to have curative qualities or the ability to confer fecundity. The stone boat of Saint Avoyé, who arrived on it near Auray, was placed in her chapel of Pluneret and came to be regarded as possessing healing powers, particularly for children with walking difficulties. At Plounéour-Lanvern, a menhir long used for fertility rites was said to have been the mast of Saint Eneour's stone boat. Others served as artefacts for oath-swearing, with terrible penalties for those who did not keep their faith. Saint Lunaire's stone had been thrown overboard by sailors lightening their vessel's load in a storm and it sank to the bottom of the sea. When the saint arrived on land, two doves brought him the stone from the ocean bed and it later became a focus for the swearing of oaths. Anyone giving false testimony before it would be dead within the year, just as someone swearing an oath dishonestly on Budoc's former stone boat was likely to be stricken by paralysis. So stones begin to weave their own stories and become subject rather than prop.

To come back to that modern granite boat. It is a thing of great beauty, tactile and aesthetically pleasing. At the time of writing it's stationed outside the cathedral in Dol-de-Bretagne. The patron saint of that glorious building, Saint Samson, is depicted there in a wonderfully anachronistic stained glass representation traversing the Channel in a little wooden castle complete with turret. I don't know how long the *Maen Vag* took to make, but I'm guessing many times longer and with considerably more man-power than using a few bundles of light, waterproof reeds and some skins. Or a wooden framework. But let's not spoil a good story, and stone boats certainly provide many of those.

6 Surround

The sea came out of stones and stones came out of the sea. Now they are locked together in an eternal battle of attrition. Brittany is almost surrounded by water, and the relationship between land and ocean continues to be fought out to this day along the vast, tortuous coastline, with giant-sized chunks of sandstone and granite carved coves and cliffs eagerly devoured by the waves. Water levels have risen considerably since the neolithic period, leaving some megalithic monuments both in and out of water, like the memorable *allée couverte* on the sand at Guirnivit near Plouescat, or one of the two semi-circular stone monuments on the island of Er Lannec in the Gulf of Morbihan, now embracing land and sea. Water is gradually getting the upper hand all around. In territorial terms, a series of coastal structures from different historical periods reflects the need to guard such an open 'border', and the ubiquitous German bunkers of the Atlantic Wall were largely built with stolen natural coastal defences (see p.215).

The struggle between stone and water is age-old, a love-hate bond, an ancient story with endless variations. Both from the innards of earth, they make music together, soft force against hard fragility, the *wu-wei* of eastern tradition, but neither stone nor man have the final answer to water. It is the essence of life on earth, as well as potentially the ultimate death of stone. The first people to settle on the land in Brittany placed standing-stones near sources to acknowledge their debt and honour this vigorous force. Some think the line carvings on orthostats in neolithic graves represent water in calm or flowing form. Maybe some wavy lines of alignments replicate streams, created in stone to honour the sinuous movement of water in a less fluid material. Menhirs in hidden river valleys are often the most memorable of all.

I shall never forget my first discovery of the off-the-beaten-track stones of **Lespurit-Quélen** (or Ellen) on the border between Peumérit and Plovan in Pays Bigouden. The site is only accessible on foot and feels like a lost secret world. Beside the stream in a wooded dip a huge menhir rises to 7m, accompanied by a substantial lying stone and overlooked by a rugged outcrop of granite which might once have been the source of material. Despite its size there was no intention of the stone(s) being seen from a distance, as they lie low in this magical place, intensified by the enclosed setting and the flowing stream, thrumming with the sense of harmonious connection between stone and water in a hidden grove. It offers a memorable sensation.

But in a contest there is no doubt that water will always emerge victorious. Malleable and driven, it can wear stone down over time with nothing more than individual drops, or overwhelm buildings with one single surge. The Celts acknowledged that power and danger with their reverence for springs and rivers, as we know from the archaeological record of finds such as ex-voto offerings (weapons and jewellery), and inscriptions indicating the propitiation of water deities for crossings of that capricious element. But they also acknowledged the healing potential of springs with their mysterious origins, and this was something that early Christianity was to exploit rigorously in Brittany with the arrival of the Breton saints, and to appropriate for their own tradition, as we shall see.

Ice melts, waters rise, land disappears. Infallible tide defences do not exist and man is impotent in the conflict, as we are learning to our cost even today. The seminal Breton Atlantis legend tells this story. In the **Bay of Douarnenez, the city of Ys** was constructed, a triumph of man's ability to build against nature, an urban centre on the sea bed itself, protected by locked gates and stone walls so thick and high that its people lived without fear, dry and surrounded by the swell of the ocean at high tide. The bay is a large shallow expanse of water sheltered between the arms of the Crozon peninsula and Cap Sizun, overlooked by the heights of Menez Hom, one of the seven sacred hills of Brittany. The tale of Ys can be seen as a clash of values between established Celtic society, where women had considerable freedom, and the incoming male dominated Christianity.

For years the walls of Ys withstood nature, untroubled. Inside the population danced and sang, the church bells tolled, and Dahut, daughter of King Gradlon, held court with her lovers and servants. She had persuaded her father to create this domain for her, away from the strictures of his saintly advisors Saint Corentin and Saint Guénolé in the capital city Quimper, where life was dull. The portrayal of her independent lifestyle is turned to one of debauchery by the Church with its more limiting values. This confused tradition has a godless city on one hand and the sound of church bells from the lost city echoing up from beneath the waters of the bay (to this day) on the other. Legend is torn between a den of iniquity in the Christian version and a scene of transformation in less moralistic versions, where the power of water is personified into deities and spirits deserving of respect.

First things first: the debauchery of Dahut had to be punished, a young woman who dared to dance and indulge her physical passions without restraint. The Devil is a useful agent in this sort of circumstance. Even though he is a Christian creation, his presence symbolises the pagan licentiousness that presumed to stray over those tight boundaries of the early Church. So when he appeared, Dahut invited the Red Man, for so is the Devil known in Breton, to share her entertainment and finally spend the night with her. He cunningly persuaded her to reveal the secret of the sluice-gates that kept the town safe. Conveniently, her father and his favoured saint Guénolé were on a visit to Ys, and as the king slept, the keys of the city's defences were stolen from around his neck. The gates opened smoothly and the ocean began to penetrate the city streets, to creep up the house walls and fill the breathing spaces of the inhabitants, until the alarm was sounded and all tried to flee.

King and saint had the advantage of strong horses which plunged ahead through the rising waves towards the shore. Dahut called to her father for rescue and he pulled her up behind him, despite the urgings of his companion to throw her off into certain death by drowning. Gradlon's mount soon began to labour under the weight of two humans. Guénolé repeated his holy command and finally the king obeyed, pushing his daughter down into the foaming waves, crying as he reached safety just as the city of Ys finally disappeared beneath the waters. Whose wickedness is punished here? Dahut floated rather than drowned, carried into a new watery kingdom somewhere other than death, where the transformative power of water changed her into the sea spirit Ahès, for a new lease of life in the world of Breton legend. Gradlon and Guénolé soon moved on to Rumengol, as we have seen. The contrast between two world-views is apparent, and this story is very differently told, according to the teller.

But there are tales of stones that have power to stop the might of water or to call it down from heaven. The idea of destruction by flood occurs in a quite different story from **Combourg**, far away in the Marches of Brittany, a border region in the east long fought over between Breton and Franks, then French. The splendid château there became the home of literary great François-René Chateaubriand's family in the 18th century and his biographical work *Mémoires de l'outre tombe* immortalised the building and its location, the setting for his 'invention' of teenage angst. '*In the woods of Combourg, I became what I am*' he famously wrote. There may also be Arthurian connections: the Coëtquen family, owners of the castle from the 16th to 18th centuries, sported the blason of Lancelot du Lac, a Breton knight by origin. (See also p.53.)

At Combourg, according to legend, a small white stone once saved the town from destruction by water. The **Fontaine de Margatte**, today on the edge of the fishing lake called the Étang des Maffins, is at the heart of the story. It lies a little distance from the great château that looms over the community. This was built originally in the 11th century on the orders of Ginguené, Bishop of Dol-de-Bretagne, as a crucial link in the defences of the fiefdom of Dol. He entrusted this stronghold to his brother, Rivallon. Not long after he was established as first lord of the new castle, Rivallon was riding outside the walls when he caught sight of a gnome-like figure struggling, with his beard caught in a bramble bush. He immediately dismounted and helped the little man get free, and in return was shown a magical stone with strange powers. If thrown into a nearby spring, it would stop the flow. They parted with mutual expressions of gratitude, but this useful tip made little impression on the great noble then, and he went on his way.

He was to remember much later, after a less fortunate encounter. He came across an old woman on the path and refused to make way for her to pass before his horse. She cursed him, calling on the waters of this very spring of Margatte to rise and flood the whole town and destroy Rivallon's château. As the waters began to surge uncontrollably, Rivallon remembered the white stone and rushed back to the spot where he'd met the gnome to find it. It seemed so tiny and insignificant in his hand. Could such a small object achieve the extraordinary feat of saving Combourg? Reaching the spring with difficulty, he hurled the stone in and the inundation began to ebb immediately. Soon all that was left at the foot of the castle mound was the famous lake given the name *Lac Tranquille*, by the illustrious Chateaubriand, whose family descendants still live in the château today. The lake remains and the spring of Margatte can still be seen under a metal grating. The white stone may still lie deep in the ground there. Who knows?

The **Fontaine of Barenton** lies in the Forêt de Paimpont, north-west of Rennes. This beautiful forest has been claimed by interested local parties since the 19th century and more recently by the tourist industry as the fabled Arthurian Brocéliande (see p.54). This legendary grab does not detract from the fact that the forest of Paimpont is a breathtakingly lovely, not to say enchanting place, full of atmospheric sites, not least of which is the spring of Barenton. It is situated not far from the hamlet of *Folles Pensées* (mad thoughts), ever associated with the rogue monk Eon des Étoiles, who established a cult here in the 12th century. He seems to have become obsessed with his own persona, believing himself to be a reincarnation of Christ, although this was somehow warped into licence to loot abbeys and churches, and live a debauched lifestyle with his followers in the forest. Interestingly, at his eventual trial, he was spared death on account of mental fragility, an enlightened view for the time.

The most common approach to the spring is a lengthy trail up through the forest from the Fairies' Mirror lake, leading by narrow paths to its isolated location. Here the source is directed down the incline by a stone channel, but it is the large flat stone at the head of the *fontaine* that captures the magical power of this place. It is said that sprinkling drops of water from the source onto it will summon up a storm of great violence. The stone is covered with offerings to this day, from acorns to candles, love tokens to crystals. Whether all the donors are looking for a little rain in their lives is questionable, although the weather ritual is still enacted here in times of drought, but it has come to be regarded as a stone of power, a conduit of universal energy thought capable of aligning with human wishes through ritual. The essence of magic.

Fontaine de Barenton

The *Fontaine de Barenton* is first mentioned c1170 in Wace's poem *Le roman de Rou*, in which he indicates the large stone's capacity to stir up an elemental furor when splashed with water. In the same period, Chrétien de Troyes used the scene for the clash of the knight Calogrenant and the fiery warrior Esclados who lived nearby. Calogrenant sprinkles water on the stone and a massive storm begins, only to stop suddenly. And then in that unexpected moment of quiet and calm, his opponent gallops into the clearing and batters the Arthurian knight into an ignominious surrender. It falls to Yvain, the Lion Knight, and cousin of Calogrenant, to avenge this humiliation. He follows the same procedure to call out Esclados, and mortally wounds him. Entering his enemy's castle with the aid of a ring of invisibility given him by a servant girl, Yvain goes on to marry Esclados' widow, who has no idea what he has done, but makes him the new defender of the *fontaine*. It's worth noting that a contemporary Welsh text *Owein, ou le conte de la dame de la fontaine* locates the Fontaine de Barenton near the sea, so maybe somewhere else altogether...

Rain-making stones have been a feature of many cultural traditions from Australian Aborigines to Japan, to the Apaches in Arizona. In a tradition of Californian tribes, water was gathered from special springs and then thrown onto the magical rock, just as the practice at the Fontaine de Barenton. Ancient Rome had its *lapis manalis*, a rain stone kept outside the Porta Capena and carried in to the Senate House for the *aquaelicium* ritual to cause rainfall by pouring water over the stone. This stone, like that of Barenton, was not associated with any specific deity or divine power, but may have been a vessel of sympathetic magic with the water shaken or sprinkled from a hollow in its form. The rituals of hot countries for rainfall in times of drought is hardly surprising, but Brittany is rarely short of a drop of rain or two. (At the time of writing in August 2022, we are actually suffering a genuine drought, hard though it is to conceive.) The Barenton legend calls down a storm of titanic proportions, which can endanger the surrounding area. Firmly fixed in the popular culture of Brittany, it also does not require a priestly intervention from a shaman or *pontifex*, just the force of individual intention.

Using stone for surrounds framed and protected the springs, creating the myriad of *fontaines* that still exist in the Breton countryside, drawing attention to these powerfully curative sources. The age-old knowledge of water's healing power became formalised in this way. They range in structure from simple rough stones, like the wild, natural source of Barenton, through Flamboyant Gothic examples such as the handsome multiple outlets at the church of Saint Nicodeme at Plumeliau, to ornate Renaissance buildings, almost mini-temples in their own right, a testament of developing architectural values in the region over many centuries. The springs usually had chapels built near them to christianise a site which may earlier have been a focus for pagan rituals, and may already have been marked by a menhir or stele from earlier civilisations. With the coming of the Church, sites soon came to be associated with an individual patron saint who 'specialised' in certain maladies for healing practice.

The stone walls were the container of sacred water which was blessed by a priest, a ritual renewed at the Pardon or saint's special festival each year. The spring could be 'recharged' by dipping the holy relics (saints' bones) to give an essence of sanctity, and make the divine power superior to that of the water alone. This was what was said to give the *fontaines* their healing capacity: the holiness of the saint, a conduit of God's power, diluted in the water. In addition to containing the spring itself, there might be other basins or containers like sarcophagi for those seeking cures to lie down and immerse themselves in the water. This combination of touching stone and water at the same time was a potent one, and these sites provide a harmonious intimacy of the two elements. It was also common practice to steep clothes or pieces of cloth in the *fontaine* to take to the home of someone too sick to travel for some distance healing. On another practical note, *lavoirs* for washing clothes were also often attached to the side or in front of the sacred space to take advantage of a flow of water.

The separation of man and nature by the Church's insistence on God's domination over the land began in western Brittany with the arrival of his representatives, the evangelising saints, in the Dark Ages. They used their apparent power over this essential element to demonstrate the superiority of what they offered. Tapping the ground or a rock to produce a new spring of cool, clear water or using the water of an existing source to perform healing, the stories of the saints are full of water manipulations. These reflect a crucial element of control that inspired awe in the people and became a factor in acceptance of the new religion.

Saint Ké (perhaps the Arthurian Kay) was a monk from Ireland who arrived near Perros-Guirec to a hostile reception from the local washerwomen. They were frightened by his sudden appearance in a stone boat and thought he must be a demon, so beat him with sticks of broom and left him bleeding on the shore. He prayed to the Virgin Mary for help and she caused a spring to flow beside him to assuage his wounds, which were miraculously cured. The water later enjoyed a wide reputation for its healing powers, and it still exists to this day near the shore of the town taking his name, **Saint-Quay-Portrieux**. The current *fontaine* dates from 1862, replacing a much earlier version. It is built of chunky granite blocks and has a strange elongated pyramid top, like a little spaceship, above the source. An inscription in very small letters on the side tells the story of Saint Ke's arrival. The saint's assailants were full of remorse after seeing the miracle of his recovery and soon begged his forgiveness for their violent welcome. This story is important, and reminiscent of the topical question of immigrants arriving over water. Together with similar tales concerning other holy men elsewhere in Brittany, it indicates that strangers were not always welcomed with open arms, and Christianity had work to do with local populations to convince them that no threat was offered.

A more active sourcing of water can be illustrated in the journey of Saint Pol, who came from Wales to evangelise Armorica, as Brittany then was, in the 6th century. After an interesting sojourn on the island of Ouessant (see p.6), he crossed to the mainland and worked his way east to the spot where his eponymous town Saint-Pol-de-Léon stands today, and the nearby Île de Batz, where he built

Chapelle de Prad Paol

a monastery. On the long migration he had to provide water for his travelling party of monks as they looked for a place of permanent settlement. Pol is said to have crossed the **Aber Wrac'h** by the extraordinary and immense stone bridge called **Pont Krac'h** or **Pont du Diable**, which is 'dated' anything from Celtic to late medieval, so he used whatever version was in place then. There is a very old monolithic cross at one end of the causeway, indicating an ancient route.

The enormous structure vanishes from view completely at high tide and is then slowly revealed by the ebbing water hours later. On the hillside above the estuary is the site of the exquisite chapel now called **Prad Paol** (Paul's meadow). Here the saint struck the ground with his staff to elicit a cool, fresh spring for his thirsty followers to drink their fill. The idea that saints appeared to know where resources lay underground makes them early water-diviners and dowsers, with the heightened senses that implies, something that ordinary people would have respected. But this is clearly an ancient site, long pre-dating Christianity. There are three springs, one under the altar of the little chapel, and two Iron Age steles also mark the spot. In another version of the legend, the saint was victorious over a marauding dragon and decapitated the beast: a spring appeared at each bounce of the severed head.

Some springs were thought to derive powers of divination from their association with saints. The famous **fontaine of Saint Efflam** is still much in evidence today. He was an Irish prince who wanted to devote himself to the religious life but was forced by his status into an unwanted marriage. On the night of the nuptials he deserted his bride, Enora, leaving the castle and taking a boat for Brittany. He arrived on the shore at the Lieu de la Grève, near Plestin-les-Grèves in Côtes d'Armor, and established a hermitage. He also placed a cross in the bay to help pilgrims crossing the vast expanse at low tide, in the days before the road was built, and the sandy route was hazardous. As well as the encroaching sea, robbers with their stronghold on the height of Grand Rocher, a steep mound overlooking the bay, might rush out and attack travellers. This ancient cross is said to be the one destroyed during American naval manoeuvres in 1944, and the current one, quite difficult to spot even at low tide, is a replacement.

One day Saint Efflam came across King Arthur in the course of fighting a huge dragon. Arthur was unable to vanquish the beast and was exhausted, badly in need of refreshment which Efflam provided by striking the ground to produce a stream of fresh water. The holy man went on to save Arthur's bacon the next day by approaching the dragon in his lair on Grand Rocher. Here the saint, cross held high in front of him, commanded the monster to hurl itself from the top of the cliff. Powerless to ignore this divine order, the beast obliged. The long red rock at the foot of the hill is said to be its petrified tail. The tradition is not one that reflects particularly well on Arthur, who is often an anti-hero in the Breton tradition, but the saint triumphant is a much more common and satisfactory theme in local terms. This legend in many versions, its interpretations and subsequent literature inspired by it would fill a book all on its own.

The *fontaine* of Saint Efflam is situated on the shore today below the chapel (rebuilt 1888) which displays on the exterior wall small statues of Efflam and Enora which once adorned the sacred spring. For Efflam's jilted wife followed her husband to Brittany and established her own little hermitage near his, devoting the rest of her life to solitary prayer. They are said to have died on the same day. The setting of these sacred structures by the beach on this enormous bay is very attractive, and fresh water from the source still finds its way to the sea. The solid four square granite structure, topping the spring like a little pavilion, has an elegant slated schist dome. Openings on three sides give access to the main basin, and the water moves on towards the beach 25m away through a three part channel. This spring is famous for its powers of divination on various subjects. Parents with a sickly child would throw in its little vest: if the garment sank, the worst outcome was likely. This seems a particularly harsh judgment with the increased weight of wet fabric.

More common are the rituals involving pieces of bread. Two pieces representing sweethearts should float along the channel close together if the relationship will last. If one gets snagged up on the way, the signs are bad. Three crumbs for a married couple and suspected lover will indicate if the suspicions are correct if the third piece moves towards the other two. Many young girls came to float bread to see if their partner was faithful, hoping not to see the morsel sink, or throw in a needle to see if they'd marry within the year. It may also have been a place of healing, as some think the name Efflam made the saint good for curing inflammatory diseases. Those seeking his help in any way would doubtless come primed with offerings, for which a stone receptacle bound in iron stands at the foot of the steps. Here pilgrims on the *Tro Breiz* (pilgrimage around Brittany) or Compostela trail could pay their respects with a coin or two, or sailors about to embark ask the saint for safe passage at sea with a token of entreaty.

The healing aspect of *fontaines* was extremely important in times when few had access to doctors, and medical knowledge was meagre. This applied especially to rural society where the need for aid was strongly felt and the old saints, who were regarded with both reverence and affection, provided a short cut to God's powers, through invocations, rituals and offerings. There was much concern with children's ailments, for obvious reasons, and common illnesses like headaches or the problems of a humid climate, with rheumatism topping the list. The blind Saint Hervé was even a specialist in mental problems like depression and anxiety. I tried out the efficacy of Saint Maudez, known for curing shingles, at his beautiful spring in Plouyé. No luck on that occasion.

The miraculous **Fontaine de Saint Goulven** in north Finistère is a good physical example of all aspects of a healing *fontaine*. Dating from 1652, it has an imposing large square granite enclosure, with a full-length covered stone sarcophagus built into the wall to one side of the main basin. Here those suffering from kidney or back complaints could soak themselves fully. A statue of Goulven himself stands in a large niche, overseeing the whole site. There are also stone benches to accommodate visiting pilgrims and those seeking cures, and a stone slab on its side tops the entrance to keep animals out. The water is then brought by a channel to a large *lavoir* or washing-place. Early postcards show Breton families sitting round this with piles of clothes waiting to be washed, an indication that the *fontaine* was not only of religious significance, but a practical and social hub for the villagers.

The origin of this spring is said either to have come from the saint himself or his parents, Glaudan and Gologwen. They had come to Brittany from Great Britain when Gologwen was heavily pregnant, but according to a *Life of Goulven* written in the 13th century, they could not find shelter after landing and were turned away by a peasant they asked for help. Echoes of a bigger story there. Gologwen therefore gave birth in a sheltered grove, but they needed water for the baby. Glaudan went off in search, but in his absence Gologwen prayed for help and was answered with a gush of sweet water from the earth, making the vital element God-given. This very spring later became sacred to her son Goulven, who would go on to become Bishop of Saint-Pol-de-Léon and a revered Breton saint. On the fourth Sunday in July, the Pardon is held and the relic of an arm-bone, acquired by the chapel in 1503, is plunged into the water by the priest. Goulven seems to have been a bit of an all-purpose healer, said to be efficacious with fever, rheumatism, eye problems and even animal illnesses, although there were other saints who specialised in the latter.

Saint Gildas and Saint Tugen were both renowned for their efficacy in treating rabies, which led to a curious custom. If bitten by a rabid dog, the sufferer should look into the waters of the *fontaine*: if they saw a dog reflected back at them, it was bad news. It was in the 18th century that this terrible disease was brought from the east and it presented a very serious threat to men and animals before the development of medical treatment. An infected dog might be suffocated between two mattresses to avoid anyone being bitten. At **Magoar**, however, deep in the countryside of Côtes d'Armor, a priest is said to have observed that an infected dog got better after drinking from the **Fontaine de Saint Gildas**, and urged other owners to come along for preventative measures. The result was many dogs being led in procession at the Pardon of Saint Gildas at the end of January to the spring just outside the village, to be blessed for protection against this danger. The story goes that so many dogs in one place led to a complete loss of order and fighting frequently broke out, sometimes to the death. The solution proposed was that a special hole should be made in the lavish stone surround of the spring before the statue of the saint, so the dogs could be fed to temper their aggression as (supposedly) a full dog doesn't fight. This became known as the *Toul ar hi* or dog hole. Disappointingly, the only hole I could see, apart from rectangular basins carrying the spring water, was a small round affair which would barely fit a tin of Pedigree Chum, and to be honest I think dog-owners may well be sceptical about the idea of offering food to stop an over-excited pack of dogs from savaging each other. After the vaccine for rabies was discovered in 1885 these rituals gradually died out officially, but the water of the spring retains its reputation and local rumour has it that a dog recently receiving a death sentence from the vet drank from the *fontaine* and lives on… At **Saint-Tugen** in **Primelin** with its beautiful church dedicated to the eponymous saint, there is a proper big round stone bowl for dogs next to the *fontaine* – neatly planted up with flowers last time I was there.

The island of **Saint-Cado**, joined to the mainland by a bridge over the Ria Etel in Morbihan, is a wonderfully fluid example of the relationship between stone and water, and the site is doubly evocative with the tide mounting. The rise and fall of the calm estuary punctuates the life of this little isle, the saint's chapel and his *fontaine*, enshrined in stone on the shore, which is sometimes bare and dry, sometimes filled with salt water to mix with the sweet source tucked into the embrasure. Steps descend to the basin with entrances on either side and the granite shrine is covered with a rounded vault, especially boat-like when viewed from the terrace above. The ridged roof is topped by a fairly recent Celtic cross; below, a modern statue of the saint (2013) looks out over the water. The whole has been elaborated and re-worked over time, from 18th century origins to much 21st century restoration.

Cado's name comes from the Celtic root *Kad* or combat, so he has not surprisingly become associated with practitioners of the Breton sport of *gourenn*, a form of wrestling. Before a contest they would immerse themselves in the waters here for strength and resistance in their bouts. But the saint is better known as a healer of deafness and headaches. The chapel on the island above the spring was originally founded by Benedictine monks from Quimperlé in the 11th century on the site of Cado's hermitage, with some considerable remodelling in later years. Inside is a famous stone called the **Lit de Saint Cado** (bed of Saint Cado). This structure of stone blocks, clearly designed for those on the short side and not in need of a comfortable night's sleep, has a sort of raised 'pillow' at one end. In the base is a rectangular cavity, ready for those seeking relief from hearing difficulties to insert their head and place their ear on the floor slab inside the hole. Some say that an essential element of the ritual is to first sprinkle holy water from the *fontaine* on the afflicted part, thus partnering water and stone for the cure. The contortion required for this act of faith is no more unappealing than stretching out on the saint's bed and placing an ear on the rigid stone pillow for a night. Although, if it worked… And seekers had to continue the ritual until they could hear the sound of the sea. Cured!

Cado, founder of the monastery of Llancarvan, arrived from Wales, in the 6th century, settling on this then deserted island near Belz where he founded a small religious establishment. First he cleared the territory of snakes and they have never returned, a feat also attributed to Saint Maudez on his eponymous island off the north coast of Brittany. But after a time, as more and more wanted to hear Cado's wisdom and took considerable risks in crossing with the changing tides, easier communication with the mainland seemed desirable, but he had not the means for such a major construction. Soon after the conception of this project, the Devil came to Saint Cado and offered to build a bridge for him in a single night, on condition that the first soul to cross it would be forfeit to him. Cado agreed, but when the Devil positioned himself ready at the land end of the newly completed structure for his payment, the saint started to cross but then produced a cat from his robe and shooed it over ahead of him. When the Devil cut up rough at this trickery, Cado launched himself ready for a fight, but his opponent leapt away, leaving only the mark of his claw on a nearby rock. (This story is told of the origin of other bridges in Basse Bretagne.)

We have already seen at the beginning of this chapter the

Venus de Quinipily

creation of a female divine spirit, when Dahut was transformed in the waves that destroyed her city. We will end with another deity, who has proved remarkably resistant to the destructive potential of water. The statue known as the **Venus de Quinipily** is a real curiosity, now placed on top of a *fontaine* with a giant granite basin near Baud in Morbihan. The garden in which it stands belongs to the ruined château of Quinipily, once the possession of the counts of Lannion, who were to play a major part in her story. But when did that story begin? Learned and popular opinion has long been split over the origins and identity of this figure of a naked woman, standing 2.15m tall. Her hair is held in place by a headband (bearing the letters LIT or TIT), her hands are crossed lightly at her waist, whilst a scarf or stole hangs down and covers her genitals. She has an Egyptian air, reminiscent of some images of Isis, and a sort of acquiescent serenity in the face of her (perhaps) final resting place. Was she brought to Brittany from Egypt by Roman soldiers? (Egypt was a popular topic in the early 19th century after Napoleon's campaigns with all the cultural spin-offs that enterprise produced.)

Or does she have quite a different identity? An early 18th century inscription on the pedestal claimed that the statue was raised in honour of Venus by Julius Caesar himself when in Brittany as part of his conquest of Gaul. It is true that Caesar made much of his descent from Venus via the line of Iulus, son of Aeneas, who was himself the son of the goddess. These divine origins were useful political propaganda, one of the tools of his dictatorship in Rome. But is the Venus of Quinipily, whoever she is, a genuine relic of antiquity or a relatively modern copy? In 1836 the inspector of Historic Monuments pointed out that the noble proprietor could simply have asked his stone-mason to make him 'an old Venus', and in the early 20th century archaeologist Gustave Thomas de Closmadeuc wrote of two statues, the original and the pretender *Venus victri*.

Whatever her origins, she was first documented on a mound at Castennec above the Blavet river in the territory of Bieuzy, 10 kilometres from Quinipily. Long attended by locals who made her the object of veneration and rituals as a goddess figure, the Venus was known as *Groah Hoart* or Ancient Guardian (or *La Vierge de la Couarde*, name of the local priory), and peacefully occupied her prominent place on this old Roman site well into the 17th century. That is, until she unfortunately attracted the ire of the Bishop of Vannes, who took against such a pagan idol and beseeched the master of the château at Quinipily, at that time Claude de Lannion, to get rid of her. Locals rallied to defend the sculpture when the servants arrived to carry this out in 1661, but the noble's will prevailed and the statue was thrown into the river.

This terrible act was followed by a series of torrential rains which destroyed all the crops, in repercussion her loyal admirers said. In 1664, they fished the statue out, but it was mutilated a few years later and thrown back into the water in 1670. Two years later the count lost the power of speech after a fall from his horse, which was interpreted as punishment by the supporters of the statue. When Claude's son Pierre succeeded him, he had the statue recovered from the water again and placed it in the grounds of a newly built château, completed in 1698. This Venus emerged triumphant from the currents of the Blavet into new status, like Dahut rising from the waves transformed. Or did she? Many believe that the statue was much too badly damaged and degraded to be restored in any way, so Pierre de Lannion must have had a copy made instead. He also added the grandiose inscription mentioned above.

In fact the statue, by now notorious, was also the object of a legal tussle at that time, as the mightily powerful Duke of Rohan claimed the prize for himself because she had originally stood on his land at Bieuzy. He went to court over it, showing her worth as a figure of heritage if nothing else, but he lost and the statue remained, and remains to this day at Quinipily. Now she calmly gazes out over a beautiful wooded valley towards the large dovecote of the former château. This building was destroyed at the time of the Revolution, and two other colossal statues were found in the grounds, twin copies of a bearded figure described as a Gallic Hercules. They were shaped for use as caryatids and are now at the entrance of the Château du Plessix in Ille-et-Vilaine. I have only seen a photograph, but it is true they appear remarkably similar in style to the Venus, and may (also) have been made at the end of the 17th century.

But Venus endures, the figure of calm mystery proving remarkably durable, an eternal archetype surviving in pretty surroundings. Past the gatehouse, a flight of steps leads to the walled garden where she holds court inscrutably, high above the monumental *fontaine*. This is not in fact covering a spring, but fed by pipes from another source elsewhere in the gardens, that has now itself run dry. Some claim the basin, of unconventional shape, is in fact her original stone niche from Castennec, turned on its side. The measurements are against this theory by a mere 5 cms. There are still those today who prefer the Isis theory and propose the idea that the basin had formerly represented the tomb of her husband (and brother) Osiris. This is one of those enigmas that hopefully will never be solved. She gives nothing away, guarding any knowledge of the distant past firmly under wraps. Let us leave her alone like that, a granite figurehead of the divine feminine for all time. A story without conclusion.

7 CELEBRITY

Certain sites have acquired the status of celebrity in Brittany. When it comes to this phenomenon in stones, it's size that matters, whether the downright mass of the Carnac conglomeration or the impressive erection of the phallic Menhir du Champ Dolent. These, together with the fabulously large chamber of the Roche aux Fées, are the most celebrated examples of megaliths here. Entering natural formations into the ring, the strongest contenders are the Chaos at Huelgoat and the Pink Granite coast, both already discussed in Chapter 1. They all share an amplitude that attracts and a certain sense of the sensational implicit in that bulk, delivering a form beyond normal expectations. Value added, if you like.

Accessibility is certainly another factor in fame, as noted previously, otherwise the extraordinary complex of megalithic structures at St Just in Ille-et-Vilaine would be top of the thinking person's list, and the tallest menhir in France at Kerloas (see p.69) in the north-west of remote Finistère would join it. These two sites require more effort, as they are well off the main tourist trails. In this sense, the celebrity of 'top' sites is to the detriment of others. But as renown tends to bring such a flood of visitors that intrinsic identity is marred, perhaps geographical chance is not such a bad thing.

Big and bold is a key element of notoriety in a human or lithic context. Good publicity is also important, and travel writers have done their bit for sites on the routes popular with tourists since the 19th century, rather less for more obscurely situated stones. Well-hidden is not the first requirement for the sort of showy spectacle that appeals to modern bucket-list taste. Fortuné du Boisgobey was expecting something much more remote when he visited Carnac in 1839, anticipating lines of towering stones like huge ghosts. He found nothing like that. 'At last I was to discover these famous stones... a little disappointment awaited me.' Fashions change. Grim and silent attract a better crowd these days, and desolate landscape, although trees are widely in evidence there now despite the threat this poses to the stability of the stones, is seen as something desirable in our over-peopled world, a symbol of liberty.

People are astonished when I don't express great enthusiasm for Carnac, which is guaranteed celebrity by a bid for World Heritage status, a brand that reflects its out-of-the-ordinariness. The site has long provided an intriguing mix of folklore, romantic Celticism, and archaeological exploration. Nearly 4000 stones, mostly in rows spread over several kilometres in what now appear as separated alignments, punctuated by burial sites of various kinds, is spectacle indeed by any standards, and it is not hard to envisage the overwhelming impact of the original monument before losses to time and human needs. The very scale of the display must have been a factor in the extent to which it has been preserved, although various stages of restoration have been undertaken, most notably by Zacharie Le Rouzic in the 1930s. Certain less frequented corners like the Petit Menec and the Géant du Manio still throw up a punch of imaginative power, but it can be an unwieldy sort of place, over-managed in part and largely stripped of identity by the dense footfall of visitors and directional prompts. The more people that use – the word is deliberate – a site, the more diluted the character, the harder to look past the levelling influence of cars, signs, litter and graffiti.

The most memorable aspect of **Carnac** is surely the alignments, those long rows of stones stretching roughly east/west, which date from c4000BC, lending suggestion to the idea of a place of grand celebratory gatherings, with processions filing between the uprights. These increase in size towards the associated raised enclosure spaces at the western end, where unknown rituals were performed, making it a sort of neolithic temple, perhaps in honour of gods or tribal ancestors, given the number of interspersed burial places at Carnac. (Either that or a stadium for some kind of physical 'sport' we haven't yet divined.) Perhaps the lines represented some kind of boundaries between different symbolic spaces which had to be crossed in a meaningful order. There was in-built drama with the early sunshine inching up the rows and the setting sun flooding the enclosure with its rays. It seems not unreasonable to believe that these earliest farmers would have honoured not only the solstices, but also the equinoxes, heralding changes of season and crucial tasks in the field. In the precarious life of man c5000BC there were certain permanences in the movement of the sun and moon, the position of the stars and the changing of the seasons. The creative intention behind those stone monuments could be their attempt to emulate this dependable continuity. The raised stones outside the lines and many of the individual burial sites were probably incorporated into the overall scheme of each alignment.

As early as 1764 Count Anne-Claude de Caylus suggested that the site was earlier than the Iron Age but it was the Celtic theory that came to predominate thoughts about the origins of Carnac, particularly in the 19th century period of 'Celtomania', with few questioning a Druidic connection. Flaubert's youthful sneer that these large granite stones laugh in their mossy green beards at all the imbeciles who come to see them reflects his contempt for Celtomanes, those fanatical for all things Celtic, rather than the site, although he was underwhelmed by his own experience there. He concluded that despite all the theories of who and how and why, all that could usefully be said was that the stones of Carnac were very large stones! He too, however, believed the site to be the work of the Druids. More serious archaeological analysis was to develop during the 20th century.

It is the site's own mythology that creates the story, running through Celts, Druids, Romans, snake cults, sun worship, petrification, astronomy and astrology. Carnac has always been a hotbed of speculation for amateur antiquarians and scholars alike, and it stimulated many popular beliefs before the age of science-based study. To explain the origins of these prodigious remains, legends abound. Some derive from historical events that took place in the 1st century BC when Julius Caesar's conquest of Gaul brought Roman forces to Morbihan to subdue the powerful Vénètes tribe, leaders of a Gallic anti-Roman coalition, who not only dominated this territory, but were a naval force to be reckoned with. Caesar eventually ordered a fleet to be built on the Loire and made the exceptional decision to entrust Roman success to the sea. In 56BC these oar-powered vessels were triumphant over their less manoeuvrable sail-driven opponents in a conflict determined by the weather off the Presqu'il de Rhys. The reprisals of the victors were savage, with many captives executed or sold into slavery.

Memories linger down the centuries and squeeze themselves into the oral tradition for which Brittany is rightly famous. The heroic resistance of the Vénètes is not forgotten, such is the long arm of this process. Some said that the stones at Carnac were the remains of their cemetery, a tribute to those heroes who stood against the might of Rome. More prosaic tales describe the megaliths as the bones of Caesar's military camp, rather elaborate tent-posts in other words. As until comparatively recent times it was believed the stones were a product of the Celtic civilisation attacked by Caesar, another idea about accommodation was that Druid conventions would have needed somewhere to put up their visitors, making Carnac a sort of glorified holiday residence.

The most lasting legend has been fuelled by the power of church machinery for the sort of publicity that is an intrinsic part of celebrity. In this case it is that of a saint, whose festival still draws crowds to Carnac every year. Cornely, an early pope in 3rd century

Rome, was forced to flee from persecution and pursued by Roman soldiers until they cornered him here in northern Europe on the shores of the Gulf of Morbihan. When finally at bay, he prayed to God for aid and his pursuers were all turned into stone, their formation in files encouraging the idea of legionary formation. (There are other stories suggesting individual people turned to stone.) An important detail of the story said that he hid in the ear of an ox grazing on the plain where the megaliths stand today. This was clearly an aetiological ploy to explain his later well-established role as the patron of horned beasts (his name may be linked with the Latin *cornu* = horn) in southern Brittany, the same role as that played by Saint Herbot in the north. Animals of this type still turn up to be blessed in Carnac at Cornely's Pardon on the last Sunday in September.

For all this pleasurable conjecture, I feel that something sheer is gone at the level of the stones themselves. The longing for individual personal experience is, of course, very modern. The original ritual site would probably have been full of noise and movement and the communal sense of the people who breathed life into it. Perhaps that life is simply finite, so it is foolish to have expectations of even tenuous connection. And today's crowds are so much more collections of individual people than a group bound by shared perceptions. But there is a blandness to Carnac that is faintly disturbing, and I can relate to much earlier travellers who found the place disappointing and depressing. For them it was desolation, for me it is as if something has worn out there, and only heavy, lifeless remains linger. It's hard for celebrity to turn serious actor, as popularity in itself tends towards the one dimensional, and such a status can suck the life-blood from any stone. The alignments behind their green metal grills seem blank and pitiful, like animals incarcerated in a zoo. An association called *Menhirs libres* (Free menhirs) works for their liberty and accessibility, a release from the bounds set by the state, whilst also highlighting the importance of other, less known, sites to spread the load a little. The potential destabilising of the stones by heavy visitor traffic is something to be considered, and presumably why only very limited parts of the alignments can be directly explored.

It is still possible to get an emotional sense of all this at quiet times, and occasional intense encounters with the past are certainly felt by some here. Sadly immersion in the site is too often dissipated by the number of people, the traffic and modern housing, even outside the main tourist season. My most authentic experience was to approach the enclosure in the Kerlescan alignments from the east early one morning, moving gently uphill alone along the rows towards a barrier of stones marking the limits of an arena for whatever took place there during ceremonies or festivities. The sense of journey and final obstacle, being kept out and limited to the role of an observer, elicited a tiny thrill of anticipation to witness whatever happened there in its earliest days. The site was in use over a long period of time, presumably bringing together the population from far and wide: maybe as many as 100,000 people lived in the area that is now Brittany in the neolithic period, and trading contacts stretched much farther afield. It remains above all a memorial to that early civilisation, even if we do not know their specific intention here.

The bottom line is that Carnac remains where other extensive alignments, like Penmarc'h on the south-west tip of Finistère (see Chapter 12) have disappeared. The more modest yet stunning site of Erdeven, touched lightly by the hand and feet of tourism, yet not far from the honey-pot, provides a telling contrast with Carnac's celebrity. Plenty of powerful communing with stones to be had there.

The **Menhir du Champ Dolent** is somewhere I have visited frequently over many years, as nearby Combourg is like my second home. The stone has an astonishingly potent presence, not entirely related to magnitude, despite the relatively domesticated surroundings. When there was nothing but the menhir rising a huge 9m from a maize field, it felt intensely impressive and mysterious at the same time, a brooding symbol of survival and continuity through the ages. Later a noticeboard appeared at the roadside. In general I'm in favour of information at historical sites if it is a) sensibly placed and b) well, historical. This board showed in strip cartoon form the tale of the two brothers who fought each other until a huge stone pulsed up out of the earth to separate them and prevent fratricide. A creation story. And one that is not unique to this menhir.

Sometimes I struggle with legends when they are a substitute for reality rather than an enhancement, an imaginative interpretation of history. Not a single word on this board to say when the menhir was actually put up or about the society that felt it worth their while to do so. People may have known nothing of the neolithic in the 19th century but there is no justification for the omission in the 21st. Also there was nothing on the name Champ Dolent, which probably indicates its position on the boundary of Dol's territory as one approaches from the south, rather than the evocative 'grieving field' which is more the popular choice, with all its connotations of battles and slaughter. Recently, and about time too, a more detailed and balanced introduction to the menhir has appeared. And anyway I know a better story.

From his stronghold on Mont Dol, the Devil raged as he saw Saint Samson building the new cathedral at Dol-de-Bretagne. He tore up a great stone and hurled it at the offending edifice, striking and destroying one of the towers, before the weapon bounced off across the countryside to root itself in the soil where it now stands.

Menhir du Champ Dolent

Why is this a better story? It relates the menhir to its historical context. Dol and Samson played a significant role in the formation of the early Breton state. The Welsh monk was quite a celebrity in his way, one of the founding saints of Brittany, an eminent public figure with strong political connections locally and at the court of the Franks in Paris.

A short walk from the Menhir du Champ Dolent, in the village of Carfantin, is the sacred spring dedicated to Saint Samson, said to be the spot where he arrived in the territory from Wales. After curing the ailing wife and daughter of the local leader Privatus, he was given land to settle with his followers and begin the foundation of the original version of the splendid cathedral that stands in Dol today. The act of entitlement which so annoyed the Devil. The eagerness of the Church to associate the spring with their saint perhaps suggests that it was a site of pagan significance. It is not impossible that the original purpose of the menhir, on the nearest visible rise and alongside a natural north/south corridor, was to waymark and honour the source.

Placed so close to main roads and railway stations, near the hub of St Malo and the border with France, this enormous standing-stone has been a natural choice for film-makers and tourist brochures alike. It is a brooding, disturbing presence in misty conditions, just right for eerie murder mysteries and echoes of old magic on the small or big screen. It was the model for a polystyrene version used in a TV series of the same name but filmed in Saint-M'Hervé, 10km from Vitré. This cinematic mystique has given it 'the power of fascination' which was evident even to Thomas Adolphus Trollope, brother of the more famous novelist Anthony, during his visit in 1840.

Over time the site has inevitably been 'managed.' Hedges much too close to the stone, destroying any sense of perspective and spoiling the proportions, and more recently, picnic tables hindering any but the most basic of photos. Context matters, but celebrity often destroys it.

Trollope says that thirty years earlier (i.e. c1810) the ground at base was opened to reveal 15 feet of the rock beneath the soil, explaining its solidity of standing. He had an interesting take on the stone: 'I could fancy it anxious but unable to communicate to the successive generations who regard it with superstitious awe, the facts whose memory it was intended to guard and perpetuate.' The notion of menhir as guardian is common, of course, even today, but his concept of the frustrated mute goes a far bit further down the road towards the idea of stones being alive.

The view of Dol-de-Bretagne in the background and the agricultural exploitation surrounding the stone emphasise its unchanged presence whilst the world around has developed exponentially. For Trollope this indicates a special quality of the stone, that it has been exempted from the usual course of nature, a characteristic that can only evoke wonder and respect in the observer, taking us well beyond modern trivia to a worthy representative of true celebrity.

Facilities are needed to cope with the numbers at places like Carnac: parkings, toilets, an information centre and shop, and these are the customary trappings of celebrity for monuments all over the world. I get the sense that the wonderful **Roche aux Fées** is feeling the creep of these modern demands, that the balance of the site between monument and tourist attraction is shifting, even if the hordes of visitors that break in waves over Carnac are more at the ripple stage here. Brittany has mostly open access monuments, but cluttering the environment with extra structures is in itself a danger to the integrity of the site. Situated in the countryside near Essé, on a plateau above the valley of the Seiche, this Angevine style *dolmen à portique*, an appellation emphasising its monumental

Roche aux Fées

entrance, is the size of a house. Or a temple, some would say.

Statistics alone lend it celebrity, at nearly 20m in length and with 2m of height in the principal chamber. This has three internal 'pillars' which may designate divisions of space connected to burial rites, or be structurally necessary to support the largest cap-stones. It is aligned with the winter solstice, when the rising sun illuminates the very depth of this main room. The anti-chamber is lower and approximately 3m square, marking a veritable progression into the principal area. In the absence of direct evidence, comparison with other sites suggests the Roche aux Fées had funerary purpose, but the scale prompts additional ideas, like a ritual meeting-place or site of worship. The actual number of stones (about 41) has always been something of an inexact science, with the strange legend that, on the night of the new moon, a couple could test the durability of their relationship by each circling the monument in different directions and counting the stones. If they came up with different answers, their love was doomed. Maybe still worth a try?

The Roche aux Fées has been something of an enigma throughout its history (until recent times of experimental archaeology) because of the sheer size of the construction and the lack of similar stone in the immediate vicinity. An engraving from a work published in 1814 by Maudet de Penhouet gives a completely distorted impression of the monument with all the stones of regular size and shape, neatly fitting together to resemble a constructed hall. This image illustrates the greater liberties that could be taken before the onset of the postcard publishing business. The monument has not escaped the common fate of megaliths to be associated with the Celts in general and the Druids in particular, as the lintel stone seems so perfectly fashioned for a sacrificial table. The material used for construction appears to have come from 4km away in the forest of Theil de Bretagne, specifically an eminence called the Butte des Piqueliers. This makes the journey of the stones to their destination through forested land a remarkably laborious one, requiring hundreds if not thousands of hands and the technological assistance of ropes and rollers or wooden cages.

Without relatively modern knowledge, looking at the scale of the edifice, what origin could be more unlikely than that the builders were ethereal fairies? Not surprising then that the Roche aux Fées got its name and attracted legends worthy of its size, with tales of fairy builders, joining a well-established French tradition, where Mélusine is the best known example. She is said to have been responsible for many notable constructions, such as roads, walls and châteaux, and to have been the founder of the famous noble family of Lusignan in Poitou.

At this site in Brittany, there are layers of stories anchored on this basic foundation. The fairies were said to have built the Roche aux Fées in a single night, carrying the blocks of schist on their heads or in their aprons. Any surrounding litter of rocks is explained by them dropping the surplus once the 'house' was finished as it was to be a dwelling place for these light little people, but also to contain burials. Tricky relations between the locals and their new neighbours led to horror stories about groans of the dead echoing from the chamber and snatched babies. (The loss of many children to natural causes in their infancy gave rise to persistent stories in folklore of fairies stealing them from their cradles.) There was also the fearsome admonition that anyone attempting to destroy the monument would be dead within a year. Perhaps most interesting of all, one of the many tales brings in Brittany's own queen fairy Viviane, lover of Merlin. A wonderfully contrived notion has her coining the idea of building the Roche aux Fées to prove the existence of fairies, because no human could possibly have achieved such a feat.

On another note, a documented event in 1855 saw two Englishmen determined to pull down the rocking stone or *pierre branlante* and finally to ruin it by their efforts. This was the mighty entrance lintel which once could be moved by a man standing on top and shifting his weight with pinpoint precision. No longer. The vandals cut off a portion of the stone which completely changed the balance on its supports. They obviously didn't know the old saying that evil would befall anyone threatening the structure. Or didn't care, but sadly there is no confirmation that they met that well-deserved fate.

Can I leave this little look at celebrity without a word for the **Vallée des saints**, now one of the most visited sites in Brittany? I fear not, although the subject is controversial and regarded as something of a sacred cow, above all criticism. Conceived as a show-piece for granite, the symbolic Breton stone, and a cultural celebration of the foundation stories of Brittany, it is in essence a theme-park. Gigantic statues of Breton saints (and traditionally there are a thousand, so its going to get pretty crowded) by individual modern sculptors cover a beautiful hillside with a small hill-fort near Carnoët. A cleverly conceived tourist attraction, it provides visual entertainment and often amusement for visitors. But it is a mish-mash of history, legend, fantasy and unlicensed imagination. Leaving aside the question of artistic merit, there seems no rhyme or reason to the arrangement of statues, with well-known figures from Brittany's early days beside those whose very existence is dubious. Not every place-name beginning in Plou forcibly yields a patron saint.

Some representations are unfathomable. Santig Du, the 14th century little black (robed) saint of Quimper, an ascetic Franciscan who brought succour to plague victims and finally succumbed himself to the disease is inexplicably portrayed as a great fleshy sybarite. Saint Yves and Saint Anne stand opposite each other as patron saints of Brittany, but one is an historical figure, the other a myth from the Apocrypha. How does the casual visitor know this? Nothing gives a sense of historical perspective or the glaring dissonance between figments of artistic imaginations and genuine traditions. Never mind the quantity, feel the difference: just go down to the exquisite church of Saint Gildas at the bottom of the hill and see the genuine article.

If you don't care about such things, it's a fantastic place to visit. It reminds me very much of the Pink Granite coast, full of oddities (although man-made here in central Brittany) which can provide great entertainment. I've asked many people who have been there to tell me about it. Quite a few take away the impression that the Breton saints were giants. How extraordinary! Not one has anything to say about the history or cultural traditions of Brittany, but they have enjoyed the visual spectacle and vivid (often the word 'weird' is preferred) imaginations of the sculptors. Fair enough. I would add to that the intrinsic beauty of the stone material is worth a look for those in search of Bretonness. But in the end, this is no substitute for the inexpressively lovely statuary of Breton churches and chapels, to be visited and valued in situ. This site reflects the much less discerning world we live in, where entertainment is king and celebrity rules OK.

8 Remnant

Château de Saint-Aubin-du-Cormier

All stone is remnant in one sense or another, but we have a remarkable romantic attachment to a set of old ruins. Structures surviving against the odds that took away their wholeness and integrity, leaving destruction, abandonment, decay, neglect, shadow-selves. The reasons for deterioration range from accidental to deliberate. Times change, society evolves and outgrows the purpose of some structures like the many medieval castles of Brittany. The slighting of the castle of **Saint-Aubin-du-Cormier**, a shocking vertical slash, was an act of punishment and humiliation for its owner choosing the wrong side in the last stand of Breton freedom in 1488 against the might of France out in the Marches of Brittany, that fluid border territory that also came to lose its meaning in the new geo-politics of the late 15th century and beyond. The stark ruin of the château, however, retains its symbolism in the on-going saga of autonomy for the Breton peninsula and freedom from French overlordship (see p.202).

Many buildings have been lost through lack of means for the upkeep, families falling on hard times, sometimes to the extent of selling up to developers and stone-masons keen to get their hands on a source of stalwart material for other projects. So a tomb becomes a quarry, locals nip out at night to carry off that finely carved block that is no earthly use to anyone any more, and vandals scrawl symbols of hatred on the faded walls of a once grand house, like the Château de Coat-an-Noz (the Wood of the Night) in Loc Envel, formerly the elegant home of Sir Robert and Lady Mond. In these semi-endings we are faced with a study of the left behind, wrecks in the sea of history, guarding the memory of the past with no authentic identity based on function in the present. But Brittany is a place that thrives on such things, tradition, continuity and valorisation.

Nature and despoilers can claim equal credit for the most beguiling ruins, with their evocative missing bits. These often seem to have more connection with plants than with people, owing their upright remnants to the tenacity of ivy and brambles, vegetation which flourishes on decay, forging a new relationship with the environment in which they are sited, and harbouring precious species of flora and fauna in their undisturbed corners. Some, however, evoke pathos for the human tragedies, on a personal or grand scale, that may have led to their sad decline, like the last example in this chapter. Not all ruin is romantic: it can be cruel, reflecting violent and unexpected actions, clinging on through subsequent eras as if intent on bearing witness to history, commemorating terrible times and savage loss through its own fragmentary survival.

The remains of castles tell us much of Brittany's history, particularly the rival intricacies that seethed between France, Brittany and indeed England in the melting pot of medieval politics. The **Château du Guildo** on the Arguenon estuary may not be the best known, but it played its part in the bitter tragedy of one of the most naive or hapless figures of the time. I first came across Gilles de Bretagne and learnt his dismal story at the bucolically situated Abbaye de Boquen, where he is buried. Born c1420, he was the third and youngest son of Jean V, Duke of Brittany, sent to England aged 8 to grow up in the English court with young Henry (future Henry VI), both tutored by the Earl of Warwick. This first positive experience was cut short, but he was sent back ten years later when his brother François had become duke, to try to regain the earldom of Richmond which had once been a Breton possession. He was very popular at court there, a great favourite of King Henry, who gave him a generous pension from English coffers. But the King of France was unhappy with these strong connections and pressured the Duke of Brittany to recall his brother. Gilles' lifelong inclination towards the English was to be his downfall in the end. When Thomas Adolphus Trollope visited the area of Le Guildo in 1840, he was urged by a local to see the château on the grounds that the owner had lost his life *'parce qu'il aimait trop vous autres Anglais'* (because he was too fond of you English). Yet it was a happy place for Gilles up until the very last moment.

Situated on the right bank of the Arguenon estuary, the castle is truly splendidly located on a low spur above the water, close to where the modern bridge crosses. On the beach of the opposite

Château du Guildo

bank, the *pierres sonnantes* (see p.178) are clearly visible from the fractured walls. When the tide is low, vast salty marshes are revealed, lined with cordgrass, marsh samphire and sea lavender, home to a population of molluscs and shellfish which attracts predators like egrets and oyster-catchers, and offers a shelter to Brent geese in winter. It's a fragile environment with some precious plants, such as the rare lizard orchid and something more modest: on the theme of ruin and survival, one may accept that not all grasses are created equal, but it would be a shame to lose the pubescent oat for the name alone. This fluid world of daily revelation and concealment admirably sets off the looming bulwark of Le Guildo, and contributes to its special story.

Trollope found the prospect of the estuary at low tide 'dreary' and mentions the dangers of quicksands. For him this ruin and its setting provided a sense of wasteland with 'a degree of poetical beauty and congruity with the features of the scene in the legends they have attached to them'. Depressing place gets the stories it deserves, or the other way around? These relate to travellers' deaths in the treacherous sands, as rash attempts were often made to cross the wide river at low tide with dire consequences. It was said that the eerie wailing heard on nights when the moon was obscured came from those long-trapped bodies. From the walls of the castle, Trollope watched two women making their way over the very same sands. When they reached a channel of water, two male guides appeared and let the women jump on their backs and be carried safely past potential danger.

The castle controlled the passage of the river, whilst allowing trading boats direct access to its quay and offering good defence on the land side. These natural advantages meant the site was occupied as early as the 11th century, probably by a wooden donjon with upper and lower courtyards hugging the contours. In the early 13th century, building started all over again as the first stone creation emerged, with a double-towered entrance and lavishly decorated *logis*. After severe damage during the mid 14th century Wars of Succession, a fine metaphor for ruin in itself where Brittany was concerned, the castle saw reconstruction on a grander scale. A whole range of staff offices ran along the west wall with new living quarters for the noble owners on the opposite side of the courtyard and a great hall for formal entertaining with a view towards the sea.

At this time it belonged to Charles de Dinan, but it was later to come into the possession of the notorious Gilles de Bretagne, who had himself taken possession in 1444 of its young inheritor Françoise de Dinan, one of the richest and therefore most sought-after heiresses in Brittany. Gilles, despite being the brother of the Duke, was kept short of lands and funds, and so not necessarily the favoured suitor for Françoise. He settled the rivalry decisively, however, by running off with the eight year old, according to some accounts, although as the girl's mother was in favour of the match, it may not have been such a surprise. Through the marriage which followed he gained numerous titles and territories, including the Château du Guildo, but there was to be another more damaging consequence to his impulsive action: he mortally offended Arthur de Montauban, one of his rivals for the hand of the heiress.

Today the site, remarkably, still has open access. Who can resist the allure of a ruined castle? Especially one with such a powerful presence. Setting and scale combine to impress, with all the changing colours of an estuary situation. The best view is from across the river, or by following a narrow path near the entrance down towards the coast to give memorable views of the walls, a patchwork of original masonry from various phases of the castle's development and some heavy-handed modern fillers. The whole structure was raised on a base of schist and dolerite, an *éperon barré* poking out into the water, fortunate in its natural defences. It would have been even more impressive in medieval times without the tree cover stretching close today, an open arable landscape for the cultivation of that Breton staple sarrasin or rye and vegetables.

Approaching from the land side, the sheer scale is emphasised by the great open space of the courtyard beyond the entry towers, which look held up by large-scale pebble-dash in places, and the seemingly endless nooks and crannies of broken turrets and ancient rooms open for exploration. Smart bright red plastic explanatory panels speak not of subtle restoration, but their content helps a good sense of how the building functioned in its heyday. The curtain walls on the river side are still intact, with an accessible lookout post on top of one of the towers, giving superb views down river towards the azure sea. When the tide is low, only a thin channel of water drifts beneath these walls, a grey string across the sea of claggy mud. The eastern fringe of the castle by contrast is a line of battered façades rising high and uneven like unsightly broken teeth. A strong sun gives the curious effect that they are melting in the heat, edges blurred and ready to descend. Beyond is a marshy valley once dug out to give a bank and ditch defence that would often fill with water.

Inside the castle, the huge courtyard with a well is surrounded by the remains of a well-ordered establishment, which once contained stables and a forge, as well as a long line of outbuildings for the servants, and a large kitchen with monumental chimney. Those essentials for castle atmosphere like arrow slits, towers, turning stairs and narrow passages (and a well-preserved toilet) are also still much in evidence. The vast reception room on the north wall, facing up the estuary, indicates the very lavish accommodation for the nobility. This space, once expensively and brightly tiled, currently has a display of pieces of ornate stonework, indicating the luxurious lifestyle the château provided. Such an atmosphere was certainly characteristic of the short tenure of Gilles de Bretagne, who was known for his love of partying, a young man who surrounded himself with finery, friends and plenty of female company.

When Trollope visited in the mid 19th century, he found a mere skeleton of the outer walls and four round towers with the remains of staircases. The massive chimney of the kitchen was the only hint of interior arrangements. He did not form a high opinion of the general workmanship: inspecting the loose mortar in the stonework, he discovered it was largely clay from the estuary, often with whole shells still in the mix, so hardly refined at all. He could not shake off his impression of gloom and dreariness, especially under the influence of the stories he heard from locals about nocturnal shenanigans. There was talk of a blaze of light from the castle ruins and sounds of revelry. Lights were said to appear on the estuary itself in the darkness to lure the unwary to a cruel fate in the greedy marshes. On moonless nights, those cries of lost souls echoed along the shores, 'pale revellers' (who were mourning) 'the absence of their cold and silent mistress.' The local peasants attributed all these things to the 'demons of the sands' and not a one of them would pass by the walls of the castle after nightfall. It is certainly a spooky place in the dark.

So what of Gilles, the England supporter? His elder brother François as Duke of Brittany chose a different political path to that of his father, who had laboured to maintain neutrality in the England/France struggle, and decided to pursue an actively pro-French policy. This seemed misguided to Gilles, who constantly agitated for the opposite view. When his brother refused to give him more lands and increase his status, Gilles offered Henry, King of England, his services and use of his properties in Brittany, a provocative act in the circumstances. This infuriated his brother and most of the Breton nobles, especially the dangerous Arthur de Montauban, who was intent on revenge for the earlier slight. Accusations of intrigue were rife and Gilles was either incredibly naive or astonishingly foolish, although he clearly counted on Henry for protection.

During his regular sojourns at Le Guildo, he invited ambassadors from England to visit and received a troop of English archers sent by the English king. These suspicious activities also angered the French king Charles VII, who urged the duke to bring his brother to heel. It was only a matter of time before the free and easy life Gilles so enjoyed was curtailed. An unfortunate letter was intercepted and François decided to act, accusing his brother of treason. He was arrested at Le Guildo in the summer of 1446. On June 25th, a friend wrote to Gilles warning him of a plot and advising him to take refuge somewhere in English control (like nearby Normandy), but the very next day, as Gilles was playing an early form of tennis with his friends in the courtyard, 200 soldiers led by Admiral de Coëtivy, Pierre de Brezé, appeared at the gates demanding entrance in the name of the King of France. Gilles had the drawbridge let down and went out to speak with the emissary. He was grabbed at once and the soldiers took possession of the castle entry. They then proceeded to sack the château, even as their prisoner was taken in chains to the duke at Dinan. François, however, refused to see him.

All his properties were confiscated, as Gilles was sent to Rennes, then Chateaubriand. He finally secured an audience with the duke and fell at his brother's feet, but to no avail. As well as treason he was accused of dishonouring girls and women, being violent and dishonest. He came to trial before the *États de Bretagne* the following month. The judges refused to condemn him, but he was nevertheless kept in captivity. The incarceration dragged on for four years. Henry VI threatened to intervene to liberate him and even the King of France responded to a direct plea from Gilles claiming terrible ill-treatment, sending an envoy to negotiate his liberty. During these final delicate manoeuvres, a false letter (crafted by Arthur de Montauban?) from the English king was conveniently intercepted, proving the last straw for Duke François.

Gilles was eventually transferred to the Château de Hardouinaye (later destroyed) where an attempt to poison him failed. He was then starved, but saved from death by a peasant woman who brought him bread and alerted a monk from the Abbaye de Boquen to come to hear his confession. Finally three assassins suffocated him with a sheet, whether on direct orders from the duke or not has never been established. To avoid an ignominious disposal of the body, the abbot of Boquen came in solemn procession and took the corpse away for Christian burial at the abbey, where Gilles' simple tombstone can still be seen. That wasn't the end of the story. When Duke François, allegedly consumed with remorse, was at Mont-Saint-Michel a short time later, he met a mysterious monk who gave him a message apparently from Gilles: 'See you at God's tribunal in 40 days'. The duke died suddenly in Vannes forty days later.

And it was certainly not the end of the story of the Château du Guildo, which still stands enduringly above the Arguenon. After Gilles' death, his wife lost interest in the place. A garrison was installed in 1488 during the war that ultimately saw Brittany lose independence to the might of France. During the fighting, the castle came under severe attack by troops of the new French king Charles VIII, and the great hall, scene of so much merry-making, lay ruined. Practical reconstruction was underway only a few years later, with adaptation for heavy artillery and a transformation of the original entrance to meet the new demands of more sophisticated warfare. A hundred years later, during the last important internal military engagement, the Wars of the League, a further artillery terrace was constructed in the south west corner. Frequently under siege during this conflict, the castle was soon in serious decline. It passed through the hands of a series of noble owners, including the eminent Laval family. Le Guildo was abandoned at the time of the Revolution and used as a quarry throughout the 19th century, with the massive central courtyard at times even sown with crops like a field.

There is almost nothing in the historical record to make this castle's mark. Had it not been associated with one of the most notorious medieval Bretons, it would probably be even less known than it is today. Gilles de Bretagne was not yet 30 when he died so horribly, fifty kilometres from this spot, a potentially innocent man savagely murdered. In the long history of the château, his occupation was like the blink of an eye. But as I reluctantly leave the towering ruins, what lingers in my mind as the spirit of the place, inseparable from the physical remains, is the image of a young man playing tennis with his friends in the courtyard, laughing and joking even as the hooves of the death squad thundered ever closer.

The very different ambience of the **Fortresse de Largoët** (Argoat = wooded area) near Elven in southern Morbihan has all the key ingredients of a romantic ruin: a sylvan valley setting beside a lake, the dilapidated remains of a 15th century chapel, the quaint Round Tower with its pointed roof and crenellations, and the octagonal donjon, rising to the exceptional height of 45m. There was even once talk of the existence of a secret passageway linking the château with the *bourg* of Elven, although sadly this has never been found. And to add to these promising structural elements, impressive enough in themselves, for a few years this castle kept prisoner one of the most significant figures of English history.

The entry for visitors today passes what looks like a handsome ancient manor house, La Porterie, complete with large stone rabbits adorning the cornice, but it is actually from the early 20th century. From here a long walk through the woods builds up a sense of anticipation for what lies ahead and the final reveal of the castle site is not disappointing. The lower of the two towers, which is not open to the public, has been renovated (1905) and looks fully habitable with proper windows and pointed stonework, but the *donjon* – how incredibly high it soars! And how incredibly well made it was originally, the perfectly formed blocks of stone look directly abutted to give the smoothest of surface outline, a work of art in itself.

Passing the outer courtyard, formerly separated from the fortifications by an arm of the lake acting as a moat, the Châtelet stands guard over the inner bailey. This double-towered entrance with its pedestrian and cart gates, has engraved on its façade the ten (gold) coins of the Rieux blazon, a reference to the owner of 1461, Jean IV Rieux, who gained possession through marriage, and the wild boar symbol belonging to his in-laws, the Malestroit family. His prestigious ownership saw the heyday of the château. He was a close confident of the last Duke of Brittany, François II, and later tutor to his children. He undertook many works of improvement here, modelling the Round Tower probably on the Tour de la Connetable in the ducal château at Vannes. The Duke's daughter, Anne de Bretagne, would help with the finance to repair damage here after the War of Succession.

Once inside what is left of the walls, it is hard to tear one's eyes away from the spectacle of the lofty donjon. It is the highest such building in Brittany, and the third highest in France. Incredibly it was once even taller. Dating from the early 15th century, there are seven storeys, including the *chemin du ronde* which once connected the two towers, and attics, but these are no longer functional or accessible. Two turning stairs serve the building, the narrowest leading to the rooms of 'madame' on the first floor and her access to the chapel two floors up. 'Monsieur' had his private space on the intervening level. Each suite had a bedroom, dressing room and toilet. The children's quarters were on the highest stage of habitation.

It's a confusing labyrinth of rooms (25, with 24 fireplaces), with little sense of private life and habits, beyond the family's use of the chapel which is flanked by two oratories from which rituals within could be observed. The staircases constantly throw the view from side to side, glimpses of passageways linking the apartments and oddly angled chambers, flashes of light through the narrow slits penetrating walls up to 9m thick. The complex architecture is dazzling enough, with its intricate design, like a moving puzzle. Inside the tower are many masons' marks of all sorts – crosses, S-shapes, lollipops – and those men certainly deserve this record

Donjon, Fortresse de Largoët

of pride in their work (and the amount of labour they'd contributed). This is not to deny that there are potentially alarming cracks heavily shored up with infill or wooden framing, but the sense of powerful solidity dominates inside and out. It was this security in its heyday that led to that famous prisoner.

On the first floor is the small room, perhaps intended for archives, where Henry Tudor was detained from 1474 to 1476. The future Henry VII, founder of the most celebrated dynasty in English history, had not anticipated this kind of restraint when he fled England with his uncle Jasper Tudor, Count of Pembroke, to seek refuge with the King of France after the Lancastrian defeat at Tewkesbury and Edward IV's re-accession to the throne, leaving Henry his only surviving major rival. Storms carried the fugitives to the shores of Brittany at Le Conquet and he was to spend the next 14 years in exile here, a frustrating time of semi-captivity and long-distance political manoeuvring. Duke François II received him graciously at Vannes initially, and Henry passed some agreeable time at the Château de Suscinio on the Morbihan coast, a favoured ducal leisure spot. But reflections on the uneasy situation with the great powers of England and France persuaded the duke that perhaps he needed to organise more specific detainment of his political refugees.

Jasper was sent to Josselin and Henry to the fortress at Elven in 1474 to become the responsibility of Jean IV Rieux. It cannot have been an idyllic time for Tudor ambitions. The location was isolated, the building a genuine fortress, with small rooms not designed for ease and comfort. Society and occupation must have been severely limited, even if he was allowed any freedom of movement within the castle. The room where Henry was kept is narrow and featureless, except for its barrel-vaulted ceiling. There is no fireplace. A broken stone slab lying casually on the window ledge records this famous occupant, a deliberately artful gesture befitting the ruin. He remained there until 1476 when the duke fell ill and his council took advantage to negotiate Henry's extradition with Edward IV. English envoys were sent to escort the prisoner across the Channel, but at the port at Saint-Malo, he faked illness to delay the sailing and, when supporters arrived, managed to escape to sanctuary in the cathedral. Locals prevented soldiers entering the holy space and protected his liberty. Some speculate that the Breton he had learnt may have been a factor in this support against the hated English.

The castle at Largoët did not thrive much longer than his departure, being fired and sacked on the orders of the French king, Charles VIII, in 1490. He forced a marriage with Anne de Bretagne the following year, and in her new regal status, she supported the restoration work carried out by her tutor Jean IV Rieux, including the entranceway on view today. The castle's subsequent life was relatively uneventful. It was sold in a state of dilapidation in 1656 to Nicolas Fouquet, Louis XIV's financial main man. After his fall from grace it passed twenty years later to the Trémereuc family, whose descendants are the owners today. Not surprisingly the idyllic romantic setting has stirred the creative imagination of writers and film-makers. In 1858 it was the inspiration for scenes in a pot-boiler of a novel (*Le Roman d'un jeune homme pauvre*) by Octave Feuillet. He described the castle at first sight as a 'feudal colossus' and marvelled at the purity of the stonework. A minor skirmish of the Chouan rebellion after the French Revolution was actually fought in the vicinity, and the site fittingly featured in the 1988 film *Chouans!* as well as Claude Santelli's TV film *Lancelot du Lac* (1970). This thundering tale opens with the easily recognisable donjon on fire, and King Ban, in response to this treachery, hurling himself over a cliff (which must have been imported from elsewhere), before the Lady of the Lake takes baby Lancelot down under the still waters...

The ruins of the **Église de Lambour** stand near the river in Pont l'Abbé, capital of Pays Bigouden. Given this left-bank position, it was originally in the parish of Combrit, but incorporated into the larger town after the French Revolution. The site is marked by a squat heavily fluted Iron Age stele, once used as the base of a cross. The skeleton of the building is still elegant, although it is immediately apparent that something besides the roof is missing. The church was built in the 13th century, as witnessed by the extant remnants of the Gothic nave, and remodelled in the 16th with a new façade, bell-tower and porch added. The arcades dividing the internal space, now open to the air, rest on pillars made up of clusters of little columns with exquisitely carved capitals, decorated with leaves and flowers, as well as a lively deer and dog hunting frieze. Less obvious are the scattered stone faces, grumpy, grinning, cheeky. The stone tracery of the windows, despite some bits blocked up, echoes the skilful craftsmanship within, the whole being set off wonderfully by its ruined state. Early photographs show the church surrounded by close tall trees, and indeed invaded by weeds at floor level. But more than the sum of all its architectural details is what the surviving building represents.

The most striking thing about this beautiful relic is that its bell-tower has been truncated, leaving it topless, an open stone rectangle, and flanked only by the residual stumps of two mini-towers. This deliberate act of destruction was carried out in September 1675 on the orders of the Duc de Caulnes, Governor of Brittany. It was one of six churches and chapels in the area to suffer this punishment after the failure of the peasants' revolt, the famous Red Caps (*bonnets rouges*) Rebellion, and the building's ruined shell remains today a reminder of the terrible events of that time. What began as urban unrest after Louis XIV's finance minister Colbert imposed new taxes on tobacco and the stamped paper essential for legal transactions, turned into a veritable crusade against injustice in the countryside of western Brittany. The socio-economic grievances it aired so bloodily were early warning signs of the impetus that drove the French Revolution a century later.

In Pays Bigouden, the south-west corner of Brittany, the rebel peasants were known as the *bonnets bleus* (blue caps) according to a contemporary source, society lady Madame de Sévigné, writing with horror from her safe haven in eastern Brittany of the violence unfolding in the west. A document known as the Peasants' Code was proclaimed here from the outdoor pulpit at the chapel of Tréminou, a few kilometres away from the church of Lambour. This was an attempt to redraft the rights and duties of peasants and reframe judicial organisation to make the system fairer for the disadvantaged. There is, however, no notion of overthrowing the established order: it was a demand for justice rather than a true revolution. But the fervour of revolt was contagious and violence soon spread, with clergy often backing the peasants in sympathy with their dire conditions. It was not only property that was endangered. When the Château du Cosquer in Combrit was attacked, the noble owner was left mortally wounded. This emblematic incident later incurred the most savage of reprisals.

As the summer of 1675 wore on, events grew ever more serious. Many manors were burnt, a tactic born not so much of vengeance as the desire to destroy written evidence of land contracts and the duties owed to land-owners. The offices of the château in Pont l'Abbé, a stone's throw from the Église de Lambour, were targeted by local rebels. The struggling peasants put their hopes in a *tabula rasa* that would form the basis of fairer treatment. The impetus of the rebellion was strongest around Carhaix, where a leader emerged, the mysterious figure of Sebastien Le Balp, a *notaire* from Kergloff. At one point he had rallied 30,000 men. He apparently had wider ambitions and an eye on the port of Morlaix, perhaps hoping for contact with the Dutch fleet, hostile to France, currently in the

Channel. A letter from the governor of Morlaix suggested to the Marquis de Montgaillard at the Château du Ty Meur, where the *notaire* had acted in legal cases for the family, that the rebellion could easily be stopped simply by the elimination of its leader. Invited to the château for discussions, Le Balp was killed by a sword thrust perpetrated by the marquis' brother.

That event saw a swift collapse of the uprising. The governor of Brittany had been charged by the king with suppressing the rebellion at any cost with a force of 6000 soldiers, who were soon wreaking havoc against poorly armed and untrained peasants. Despite the governor's admission in a letter to Colbert that the wretchedness of the peasants is 'so great that we must understand where their rage and brutality lead them', there was plenty of unrestrained violence, as soldiers raped and murdered indiscriminately. The scale of reprisals was truly horrific. At Combrit, where the lord had been murdered, fourteen peasants were hung from a single oak tree. Others were broken on the wheel or sent for forced labour.

And chapels where bells had summoned the peasants to action or flown the red flag of the revolt had their bell-towers lopped off, a gesture of contempt to cause humiliation to the local populace. So the missing limb of the church of Lambour remains, by its absence, a powerful ghostly symbol of the importance of faith in Brittany and the desperate determination of local people, who were prepared to give their lives in the cause of simple justice. It is also a fitting expression of the deaf ears on which their appeals for fairer treatment had fallen. At the end of the 19th century the local council made the decision to remove the roof which had deteriorated to a dangerous degree. At that point the church was only used for two annual Pardons, so the statues were removed, taken to Notre-Dame des Carmes just across the river, and the building opened to the skies. Given its history, this action reinforced the notion of ruin as an historical symbol of identity, which defines the status of the Église de Lambour today.

A firmly entrenched tradition says that the tall, steeple-like lace *coiffes* (head-dresses) of the local women, which in themselves have become a well-known touristic representation of Breton culture, are a style deliberately developed as a gesture of 'replacement' for the lost bell-towers. It's one of those stories that sound emotionally compelling, and so garner substance, but have no basis in truth. Sorry.

After the French Revolution a hundred years later than the peasants' revolt, a new Republican official in Léon, north Finistère, threatened a priest to destroy 'your bell-towers of which you are so proud and which pretend to ascend right into the sky!' The priest replied: 'And when you have toppled them, will you then blow out the stars?' The image of blowing out stars seems appropriate for a final example of ruin and remnant. On the cliff-top of Pen Hat above the Pointe de Toulinguet near Camaret stand the gaunt vestiges of the **Manoir de Coecilian**. The house, built in 1904, was first called the Manoir de Boultous (Breton for monkfish) by Pierre-Paul Roux, a poet better known by his pen-name Saint-Pol-Roux, the owner, who moved in the following year with his wife and three children. Born in Marseilles in 1861 and very much a part of the literary Parisian scene in the 1880s and 1890s, financial straits had made him an exile, but he discovered, like so many others, the profound pull of Brittany, likening it to a 'sister' of his native Provençal. After his son Coecilian was killed at Verdun on 14th March, 1915, he changed the name of the house in his honour. The poet himself was to die of heartbreak after the loss of this home and his work at the hands of German soldiers in the Second World War.

The ruins reflect an amalgam of form and style, leaving the

Manoir de Coecilian

traces of an extraordinarily grandiose neo-Gothic building which belied the original site, where a simple coastguard's stone cottage was the only habitation, looking out over the vast fullness of the ocean. Saint-Pol-Roux employed an architect to build identical wings, each with four towers, on either side of the cottage, incorporating a traditional structure into a mammoth of granite, brick and concrete. Today it is a place of ghosts, its eerie uprights echoing the neolithic alignment of Lagatjar on the plain just behind, a place of calm and storm, inspiration and catastrophe. The remnant of a man and his own created landscape.

He lived in the house on the cliff for thirty-five years, always returning to this base from visits to friends, family reunions in the south of France or literary events. He lacked the means to spend significant amounts of time in Paris even had he wished. His wife Amélie died at home in 1923 at the age of 54, and after that sad event, his daughter Divine, who was often at Camaret, became his closest emotional focus. He had been highly regarded as a symbolist writer early in his career and wielded considerable influence over others in his poetical and theatrical writing. The remote location above the Atlantic waves was inspirational for Saint-Pol-Roux, the poet in his palace, so dramatically situated.

'Solitude is the multiplication of the self', he explained in an interview in 1937, but he was often not alone. Many famous visitors from the artistic community came to the Manoir de Coecilian – Max Jacob, Victor Ségalen, and André Breton, whose recognition of the poet brought him into the embrace of the Surrealist movement.

I first discovered Saint-Pol-Roux through his poem *Bretagne est univers*, a hymn to the Bretons and their Celtic heritage, composed in 1934. Here he speaks of Brittany 'shaping a proud domain from granite', but the implication is also of strength emerging from the rock itself. You might as well say the stone is in the people. The rest of the poem probes the richness of Breton culture, faith and endurance, its foundation in the natural world of land and sea, and its spread far and wide, with the Bretons compared to birds of the air in their number and purity.

> Ta race impérissable dont le Temps s'étonne,
> Ô Bretagne éternelle comme l'Univers!

> Your enduring race which amazes Time itself
> O Brittany, eternal as the universe!

About his manor house on the cliff, he wrote in 1922 *'Ici j'ai découvert la verité du monde'* (Here I learnt the truth of the world) and to spend time there was certainly to be fully immersed in the powers of nature and the pulsating solitude that so often leads to vibrant creativity. In 1929 he wrote to a friend of incessant storms with the house rattling and groaning, leading to serious damage that would take a year to repair. But he was also part of the community of Camaret, involved in local associations and donating money for good works like the church roof. The views of an incomer became those of an insider through empathy and passion, and the abiding spirit of place here at Pen Hat is a true combination of the vision of one man and his location, an alignment of human heart and the landscape.

But all the life and laughter, all the creative struggle and family joys or losses, were to end in murder and havoc on the lonely clifftop. On the night of 22nd June 1940, three days after the Germans had occupied the peninsula, a soldier appeared at the door of the house and claimed a right of entry. He stayed for hours, insisting that the servant Rose brought the poet, now aged 80, and his daughter Divine downstairs. Refusing all attempts to get him to leave, he finally drew his pistol and wounded Divine in the leg with a shot, then fired two bullets into the mouth of the servant, killing her instantly. Saint-Pol-Roux, in fear for his daughter's life too, wrestled unequally with the soldier who thrust him aside and assaulted the helpless woman, whose shattered leg made resistance impossible. She had no doubt that he intended to rape her, but the family dog so terrified the attacker at that point that he ran out into the night, leaving his trail of devastation behind. He was caught soon after, court-martialled and swiftly executed by firing squad.

Divine was taken to Brest hospital for sterling attempts to save the leg from amputation and months of treatment. Her aged father, himself battered in body and spirit by events, used to take the ferry across the Rade de Brest to see her every day. One evening on returning home to the great house on the cliff, he discovered that intruders had ransacked his study, destroying and burning many of his manuscripts. This attack on his very existence as a writer and the pain of the lost work proved more than he could bear. He was also taken to hospital in Brest where his daughter saw him weaken by the day. He died in October 1940, and was buried in the cemetery at Camaret, according to his wishes.

What of the Manoir de Coecilian? It was requisitioned by the occupying forces as a Commandant's post, and as such drew heavy allied bombing, causing much damage to the fabric of the building. Seven days after Camaret was liberated in September 1944, a further air strike started a serious fire in this undefended sitting target. After the war, Divine gave the house to the commune of Camaret, hoping that it would emerge from all the tragedy as a museum in honour of her father. Instead, it was left to steady degradation and the crippled state of the present day. The Manoir de Coecilian remains a ruin in progress. A symbol of a symbolist. The home of a man who was always looking out to sea.

Ruins and remnants: something in us responds to these reminders of transience, something more than idle romanticism and idealisation. Ruins make us happy and sorrowful at the same time, a potent melancholy for reflections on our own lives and situations, nostalgia for the greener grass of our own pasts. That broken arch or crumbling tower seem to pose questions about ourselves and our endurance as much as the old heap of stones we are ruminating over. An aspiration of resilience, a desire for authenticity, the pang of missing parts all draw us eagerly into the arms of dilapidation. And, of course, we know there is a story to be had, that people like us once lived, loved and suffered within, leaving us the wistful legacy of their context, the sad staying power of stone.

9 Transformation

Transformation is not only a common motif of folklore, but scientifically already in the nature of metamorphic rock, and this geological process is echoed in the adaptation of usage during a seemingly endless life. Man's enterprise always made full use of stone's properties in this context, altering location, purpose and appearance as it suited. Recycling is part and parcel of the process, and many a house and garden wall has benefited by chance from the ruin of chapels and châteaux. Something decays, something else is enhanced, it's the cycle of history. But more purposeful transformation and re-use is also common, and may involve a wider change of placement.

This practice started even in the neolithic period, with the famous example of a roof slab in the **Table des Marchands** in **Locmariaquer**, one of the larger surviving dolmens. This appears to be part of a large standing-stone, decorated with a hunting scene, and subsequently broken into three. Here can be seen the decoration of a *hache charrue* or axe-plough and a crook, and just the front legs of an animal. Another part of the same stone is to be found performing the same function in the cairn on the island of Gavrinis in the Gulf of Morbihan, although strangely upside down. On the reverse face are the rest of the animal (horned), another of the same type in entirety and another large axe-plough. The third and uppermost section of the menhir may have been used in the ceiling of the tomb of Er Grah, also on the Locmariaquer complex. Impossible to say who would have decided on these separations and second usage or why. The whole was perhaps originally upright on the same site as the Grand Menhir brisé, a fallen four piece stone which would have measured 20m in total when raised, now lying in the proximity of the Table des

Marchands. Then it too would have been knocked down, broken up and repurposed, with a part being transported to Gavrinis, which at that time of lower sea levels would not have been an island, and only three kilometres away. So change of location was a part of early recycling of material, perhaps during some renewal of the site's usage.

There are stones that are recognised in one form and then given new purpose: a Christianised menhir for example, or a stele made into a borne for a Roman road. An unusual re-use of previously worked stone can be seen in the excellent **Finistère departmental museum**, located in the bishop's palace at Quimper. An **Iron Age stele** has been transformed in Roman times into a new religious object, with relief carvings of the gods Mercury, Mars, Apollo and a female figure, perhaps Hygie (daughter of Asclepius) or Sirona (a healing goddess). It was discovered in 1868 at Kerdavol in the commune of Plobannelec, and probably once belonged to a small rural oratory. It is a unique piece in the clear transfer to a new context in Roman style. A more modest but equally telling example sits beside the D14 at **Le Runy**, between Berrien and La Feuillée. This sweet stone relic is a veritable mishmash of bits. A cylindrical Iron Age stele (or maybe even from an earlier period) was probably repurposed as a road marker, and is now topped by a cross. Long hidden in the tree-line, it has recently been starkly revealed by the cropping of a pine wood.

No-one can agree on the origins of the two curious stones known as **Babouin and Babouine** (sometimes given the forenames Jean and Jeanne) in the woods near Trédion. Estimates range from original menhirs to Iron Age steles to Roman bornes to relatively modern rude sculptures. Favourite option seems to be neolithic origin transformed in the Iron Age. Indisputably, they are two stones on which faces were once rather crudely figured. This anthropomorphism immediately renders them of significant

Babouin, menhir

interest to stone-lovers. Tracking them down can also be a fun pastime in itself. Babouine faintly reminds me of the statue-menhir of Guidel in Morbihan, mentioned in the museum at Carnac, which is a stylised figure with clearly sculpted head and shoulders (unlike Babouine) wearing some sort of coronet, and a necklace above her breasts. This was the subject of an article in 1960 by the great archaeologist Pierre-Roland Giot, who gives comparisons with other images of the 'Mother Goddess'.

Babouin, the 'male' (1.5m), is smaller than his 'female'

counterpart (2.2m) and has a round, flat disc of a visage with eyes, fat nose and a straight-line mouth. The stone does rather resemble a personified penis, supporting the theory that these representations of the two sexes are linked to fertility. The other has lost the detail of its face with weathering, but the lower protruding wedge could certainly indicate a pregnant stomach, although that would make a semi-circular engraving usually designated a 'necklace' decidedly oddly placed. It actually looks more like the remains of a smiley. There is little else to strongly indicate gender on this one. Some discern the outline of legs on the lower part, but these are not so obvious to casual inspection. The stone was shown flat on the ground in an early postcard from c1905, but Le Rouzic, curator of the museum at Carnac, raised it in 1934. Their names presumably derive from the sense of a grotesque figure (root 'bab' = lip) and not a monkey with a long face (*babouin* = baboon), but there's no evidence. Equally, the purpose of their transformation from original stone to sculpted figures remains unknown, so there is all the pleasure of a genuine enigma to be enjoyed here.

The pyramid-shaped heavily fluted stele (3.3m) in the churchyard at **Sainte-Tréphine** has not been much changed in appearance, unless you look very closely, but given a new (invented) history well-removed from its ancient origins. These granite monuments are found prolifically especially in northern Finistère and southern Morbihan, dating from 550-300BC. They are associated with funerary sites, usually where cremations are found, and probably had a generally commemorative function in Celtic society. This magnificent one is being reused for the same purpose but in a transformed context, gaining a new connection with the legend of Saint Tréphine from the 6th century AD. It stands right up against the wall of the little chapel dedicated to Tréméur, her son from the ill-fated union with Conomor, and was given the

Christian interpretation of marking the site of her death. Or rather her second death, as Tréphine had much earlier in her life undergone the shocking experience of decapitation at the hands of her tyrant husband (see p.41).

Tréphine, daughter of the Count of Vannes, had been used as a pawn in the political marriage alliance game, and given Conomor's reputation (she was his fourth wife), this new status was never going to end well for her. Eventually, when pregnant and therefore nearing her disposable date, she fled from her violent husband. He was not the sort of man to give up, however, and pursued her relentlessly. Various places claim the dubious honour of being the murder scene. One is in the Forêt de Queneçan by Lac de Guerlédan (where Tréphine also has a chapel), another is just outside Vannes, her family home. She was laid to rest there (both bits) and an urgent summons sent to Saint Gildas, who rushed to the scene and was fortunately able to provide a miracle by sticking the severed head back on her shoulders. It was the least he could do, after all, as he had urged the benefits of this terrible marriage in the first place…

Her son Trémeur was born safely and lived for about a decade, entrusted to the care of Saint Gildas' monastery, but he was eventually discovered and killed by his father when out walking in the countryside. A disaster for the boy, but wasted effort by Conomor, as it turned out the prophecy that his son would kill him actually meant to say step-son (see p.41). Young Trémeur was buried here in the village that now bears his mother's name. The chapel covering his tomb was built originally in 1577 and remodelled in 1881. Four smaller steles are placed around his resting place within. His mother in her 'second life' went on to found a convent in Vannes and lived there for many years before retiring to the place where Trémeur was buried, here in Côtes d'Armor. When she died in old age, she was buried in the church where her sepulchre can be found.

The fine stele plumb up against the exterior wall of the chapel was probably moved here from another site, and the process of claiming its status for the Church began early: a cross was engraved between the ribs and a now illegible inscription (maybe as old as the 10th century) on the west face probably reads *crux mihael* (Michael's cross). The cross once planted on the top has

Sainte-Tréphine, stele

disappeared in postcards from the early 20th century. So the monument has been given fresh significance, and been de-paganised by its new Christian surroundings, honouring a local saint in a sacred precinct. Rather than marking the grave of an unknown Iron Age chief or communal cemetery, it has become in local tradition the memorial of a specific dead woman with an important role in the Dark Age period of emerging Brittany, a symbol of goodness and innocence versus the godlessness of Conomor.

The phenomenon of Christianised menhirs, sanitised by the simple addition of a cross on the pinnacle or a carving on the body of the stone to express God's dominion and domination was widespread, especially after the strong missionary movements of the 17th century in western Brittany. Sometimes the grab is striking. **Men Marz** or the 'Miracle Stone' (see front cover) is a characterful menhir near Brignogan Plage on the north coast of Finistère. The name may be more correctly attributed to another less distinctive stone not far away, but this one seems to deserve it with an impressive 8.5m height and a quirky outline, including the all-important ledge more than half way up, which bred a popular local tradition. Young women who succeeded in lodging a pebble up there would be married (or if married, have a child) within the year. Such superstitions attracted the ire of the Church, especially in this area, part of the region of Léon, which had a reputation for strict priestly authority. A small cross was added to the top and another carved on the south face probably in the early 19th century, a mild intrusion, almost as if the magnificence of the stone limited the scale of the imposition. But for a long-standing local tradition, it was not the crosses that were the conduit of the magic, but the stone itself, huge and timeless, rearing up above the landscape, an unforgettable presence so much larger than the scope of normal lives.

One unusual attribute of Men Marz is that it is set directly on the earth, not buried at the base as most menhirs. It plays a part in stories deriving from the Dark Ages, long after its own creation, and the arrival of the Breton saints in the 5th-7th centuries. Saint Pol is the local poster boy for this area as his cathedral in Saint-Pol-de-Léon testifies to this day. A short distance from Men Marz is one of the claimed landing places where he arrived in a stone boat on the beach at Pontusval (see p.93), just along the road from the famous menhir. But he is the subject of another strand to the local tradition, which does indeed attribute a sort of miracle to Men Marz. When established as bishop in his cathedral, he is said to have received news from his sister Scifolla, who had set up her own religious house further along the coast, of flooding affecting her community. Soon on the scene, he took decisive action by planting the enormous stone where it now stands and forbidding the sea ever to encroach again beyond this marker. The sea is not generally amenable to severe ticking off, but apparently it hasn't. Yet. If the theory about Saint Pol deliberately targeting a pagan stone circle on Ouessant before crossing to the mainland is correct (see p.6), and it seems not unlikely, then his connection with the area around Men Marz could indicate another calculated visit to take over association with a remarkable local focus of pagan tradition for Christianity and the new God on the block.

The most dramatic of all standing-stone transformations is undoubtedly the **Menhir de Saint Uzec** in Pleumeur-Bodou near Lannion. Here the top third of this imposing ancient stone is covered with the instruments of the Passion in bold relief carving and a squat cross tops the whole thing off. The colourful painting of Christ on the cross that once covered the centre of the stone, visible in postcards from the first half of the 20th century, has worn off, but it must have been like an advertising hoarding for Christianity in the years after its transformation in about 1674. The

Menhir de Saint Uzec

stone is almost 6m tall, broad and solid, with deep weathering grooves marking the north face distinctively, making the back view almost as impressive for more natural reasons. The whole is set apart on a stone platform with a stepped entrance, about 500m from the chapel of Saint Uzec, and it seems likely that the changes to the menhir came as a result of the construction of this building. The detailed representations of the Passion symbols portray hammer and pincers, whips and the three nails of the crucifixion, as well as the Virgin Mary and the handkerchief of Saint Veronica, the coins of Judas' betrayal and a cock to indicate Peter's denial of Christ. But prominent representations of the sun and moon with human faces add a curiously pagan element. One of the many early postcards of this treasure makes the overall hybridisation of the stone explicit in its caption: *'monument mégalitique païen / orné d'emblèmes chrétiens / Exemple de greffe réligieuse (*a pagan megalithic monument, decorated with Christian symbols, example of religious graft). The transformation brings a pagan landmark into the framework of the Church, on a route leading to a chapel, making it part of pilgrimage, like a stage on the road towards God, or a step on the path of the Stations of the Cross. It knits the menhir into the new landscape which was being fashioned by the imprint of Christianity.

Amazingly, some transformations are even more determinedly elaborate. High above the Blavet Valley is an oddity of a site at **Coët Correc**, well worth the detour from Lac de Guerlédan in the centre of Brittany. A sign in Caurel points up narrow roads to a small parking area and then the climb continues on foot, winding up through woods heavy with holly amongst the oak and chestnut. Glimpses of the lake far below and rocky outcrops close at hand are little preparation for the extraordinary sight that awaits on emerging from the trees to the edge of a bright crop field. It takes a moment to realise what you are looking at: those expecting just another old alley grave get a lot more than they bargained for.

The narrow end of the large neolithic burial structure appears to be wedged firmly inside a bridge, like an accidental railway obstruction or a stone train stuck in a tunnel. On closer inspection, however, the singular nature of the more recent structure becomes apparent. A huge stepped platform has been deliberately constructed over the ancient remains, snugly enclosing the monument, in a considerable leap of elaboration for the process of Christianising a pagan relic. This astonishingly ambitious, almost hubristic effort, was the work of Mathurin Le Flohic, the local farmer, in 1904, as an extreme expression of pious devotion. It seems strange to have left the pagan monument untouched, but perhaps the amalgamation into a demonstration of Christian values seemed more powerful a rebuke. Or one could take the view that is an acknowledgement of an earlier form of attention to the dead, so ultimately a respectful incorporation of one thing into another. The neolithic structure, however, is certainly stifled by its unexpected appendage, like the significant relegation of enclosing brackets or maybe just the satisfaction of having the last word. It feels like a form of imprisonment.

For the true extent of the transformation we need to turn to old postcards, which reveal the scale of the modern adaptation. Two versions exist, from c1904 and c1910, showing that a cross with the crucified Christ on a solid pedestal once surmounted the platform and gave it purpose. Human figures in the photos give a sense of scale. The first has a group complete with tripod-mounted camera and dog posed on the top, while a servant girl waits on the lower steps. The later one has two figures on the alley grave itself, where the stones of the eastern end appear to be in disarray. To go back to the origin of the site, the *allée couverte*, probably dating to around 3000BC and constructed of local schist, has a total length

Coët Correc, allée couverte

of 16m, the chamber itself measuring 10.5 x 1.4m with a lateral entrance on the south-east face. Here two stones have been scooped out to provide a small circular porthole opening: impossible now to know why, but it grants access of a kind or a view within. The monument was excavated by Abbé Collet in 1870, when finds consisted of a flint arrowhead, charcoal and pottery fragments. The burial chamber may once have had a paved interior and been covered by a tumulus.

The place has a strangely unworldly atmosphere today, perhaps the result of its confused identity. Here two belief-systems are forcibly merged in an effort to transform the neolithic chamber into an expression of the glory of God or at least an add-on to the calvary above. On the other hand, imagining a conflict between these two representatives of vastly different values, the *allée couverte* might have had its revenge in the 1980s when the calvary fell down during another excavation. Inevitably it hit the grave below, causing some damage, but it was the end of the great cross, although some restoration of the platform that bore it has occurred.

Perhaps the greatest interest of this thought-provoking site is the beauty of the dry-stone work between the two monuments. Not much had changed in that process over the intervening five thousand years. The materials were locally sourced, and tools to shape the stone were still potentially wielded by hand. Both structures demonstrate a mastery of contemporary technique and the meticulous placing of the individual stones with devout intent, whether towards God or ancestors or cosmological powers. Now brambles and weeds sprout from the cracks between the steps, but the exquisite work of the arch in what the French call *anse de panier* or basket-work style, remains memorably impressive. Somehow the two elements here have achieved a balance of interest and durability, a religious hybrid, becoming something other in the sum of their two parts, the very nature of transformation.

The **Menhir des Droits de l'Homme** is a megalith of rather original outline and impressive height (5.5m), transformed into a memorial for a famous shipwreck in 1797 on the coast of Pays Bigouden. It was a dramatic story, immortalised here on this large inscribed stone by one of the survivors. *The Rights of Man* under Captain Raymond de Lacrosse, left the port of Brest for Ireland, carrying 600 crew and several hundred soldiers. On the way they took two English brigs with a haul of fifty prisoners, including a certain Major Elias Pipon from Jersey, who would one day be responsible for the monument. The ship then got separated from the accompanying vessels and was stuck for four days in Bantry Bay, losing two anchors. They drifted back towards France and were marooned in thick mist off the Bigouden coast when the British frigate *Indefatigable* appeared. On the 13th January combat was engaged, and after a few hours the *Amazon* reinforced the English side. The battle was fought all through a moonlit night. *The Rights of Man* fired 1700 canon shots altogether, but stormy conditions prevented them using the lower guns. It was a bloody conflict, with 100 French killed and the same number wounded. At one point they desperately attached a cable to a rock and tried to disembark. Twenty men were hanging above a turbulent sea when an English shot is said to have severed the line, and all perished in the water below. Still the French refused to yield and shouts of *Vive le République* were heard. In appalling weather and with the ship floundering, the English opponents decided to get clear and made off in different directions, the *Amazon* later getting stuck on a sandbank further north.

The next day *The Rights of Man* was still afloat but weather conditions prevented a single person leaving the ship. A rescue attempt failed dismally when the boat from the shore rammed into the larger vessel with more loss of life. It was not until the 28th of January that the starving survivors were saved after the ship ran aground on a sandbank and broke up. Altogether about 600 lives were lost. The captain wrote to the Minister of War to say proudly that all men had done their duty. Surviving the tragedy, prisoner Major Pipon was taken to Brest and then sent back to England where he rejoined the army. His own story reflects remarkable changes of circumstance. In 1840 he returned home to Jersey and then to Finistère, scene of his remarkably lucky escape from imprisonment and death. He had the menhir inscribed (words now highlighted in red) to commemorate the loss of the ship in Baie d'Audierne, and placed eye-catchingly beside the Plage de Canté.

'Here around this Druidic stone are buried about 600 shipwrecked sailors from the ship The Rights of Man, *broken by storm on 14 Jan 1797. Major Pipon, of Jersey, having miraculously escaped this disaster, came back to this beach on 21 July 1840 and duly authorised the inscription on this stone as lasting witness of his gratitude. A DEO VITA SPES IN DEO*

In 1882 a fête was held to celebrate the restoration of this former menhir, and a plaque added to acknowledge that the stone '*twice consecrated by time and history*' had been classified as an historical monument. Maybe that counts as a third transformation.

An even more extreme form of that process is when people are turned to stone. Petrification is a common theme of folklore: Medusa in Greek mythology was probably not the first, even if she is the most referenced for that skill of rendering her opponents solid and immobile. In the context of megaliths, the process is often used as a story to explain the presence of those otherwise mysterious and superstitiously revered stones. Especially if they have a rough human-like shape. Here in Brittany the notion is most commonly utilised as a demonstration of Christianity's power of punishment for sin. Girls dancing on a Sunday is a popular motif, found elsewhere in Europe, with this frivolity firmly stamped out by the priest's denunciation, leading to terrible transmogrification. This is often the explanation for circles or other layouts in lines reminiscent of Breton dancing figurations. The best known is

Les Demoiselles (the young women) at **Langon** with more than thirty quartz uprights in an oval shape with parts of outer lines that perhaps enclosed it.

Another famous revenge fixation is that of **An Eured Vein** (the Stone Wedding Party) in the **Monts d'Arrée**, where merry revellers refused to make way for a priest on the moor at night (already mentioned in Chapter 2) and his curse transformed them into a wavy line of standing-stones, interestingly placed on a plateau between the Yeun Elez marsh, which was regarded as an entrance to Hell, and the sacred height of Mont-St-Michel-de-Brasparts. At Carnac, Le Rouzic recorded the legend that a feckless young man called Minour Krifol, who had frittered away all his inherited wealth, was turned into a stone pillar by God himself and his spirit was now trapped inside the menhir de Krifol near the Menec alignment. No wonder groans were heard resounding in this area at night. I've never seen this interesting stone and apparently it is now out of sight on private property.

Natural rocks get the treatment too, with a dramatic story from the **Île de Bréhat**. Here on the north-eastern tip of the island is the Phare du Paon, not, disappointingly, Peacock Lighthouse, as the French would seem to indicate, but a lighthouse at the extremity, with *paon* being a malformation of *pan* or *penn*. Below this is an impressive chasm, marked by two pillars of rich red rock, the petrified form of two dastardly brothers, sons of Meriadec, the Count of Goëlo. These young men soon squandered the wealth he had bestowed on them and were greedy for more. So they raided the Abbaye de Beauport, for which blasphemous act their father had them imprisoned. But they quickly escaped and vowed to have their revenge on him. Meriadec first took refuge in the abbey and then made use of a secret tunnel which led all the way underground to Bréhat. He carried with him the monks' most precious valuables, as his sons were once again set on attacking the religious house.

When they found their father gone, however, they furiously pursued him to the tip of the island, where he could run no further. They slaughtered him there and then, his blood staining the rocks their distinctive colour. But before they could get their hands on the gold, they felt themselves suddenly rooted to the spot, then unable to speak or breathe, until all that could be seen were their petrified silhouettes.

And not only people, but animals. Paul Sébillot (1843-1918) in a collection of folklore from Haute Bretagne records an initially promising story of the legendary **Roche aboyante** (Barking Rock), but it turns into a rather banal example. Saint Convoyon, founder of Redon Abbey, was accustomed to visit Saint Fiacre near Bains-sur-Oust. They would sit together merrily chatting in the countryside, but were one day disturbed by the incessant barking of a dog. No amount of exhortation or command would silence the beast, so they cursed it and the poor thing turned into stone. The end. If the rock continued to bark on occasion, reflecting its hybrid nature, it would be more interesting, but sadly there is no record of this. The tale hardly reflects well on the two saints, who were chronologically incompatible anyway, and presumably springs from the shape of some stone (called a menhir in the text) or a weird noise it made in the wind, although I know of no trace of it on the ground. This is probably one of those very localised legends, where a native grows up knowing the detail without consciously ever having heard it, a story imbibed at birth on the breast.

Something more concrete, as it were, can be found in the churchyard at **Lanrivoaré** (the holy place of Saint Rivoaré or Riwal, a 6th century evangeliser from across the Channel) only a short distance from the hermitage mentioned in Chapter 3. And it is a unique thing. Here beside the church, a rectangular enclosure is paved with uneven slabs, looking not unlike crazy-paving, and at the eastern end sits a granite niche, topped by a cross and containing a statue in poor condition. Many claim this to be Saint Hervé but it looks to me like God holding Jesus, with something hovering, a basic representation of the Trinity. In front of this on the ground is a long stone tray bearing seven stone balls of varying sizes, but resembling in shape the loaf known as a *boule* (ball). The smaller ones are more like bread rolls, to be honest. And these stones are said to be the petrified version of newly baked bread, when Saint Rivoaré (or his nephew Saint Hervé, according to other accounts) punished the baker who refused to give some of his wares to help the poor. These sorry specimens remain here on display as a reminder of what happens to those without charity: their edibles turn into minerals.

But that's not all. A stone altar stands on one side of the enclosure with a very curious raised oval-shaped engraved blazon, apparently of two 16th century families, and a striking carved bearded head with a hat on, which may be a saint but has a decidedly pagan air. This really is a most unusual site. The whole ensemble, which is entered down steps, past a granite Iron Age stele (1.2m), so emphasising its separate and significant identity, is known as the **Cemetery of the 7777 saints**. It is supposed to commemorate the massacre of the early Christian community here founded by Rivoaré, and wiped out by pagan opponents. It is true that there was plenty of local hostility to the incomers of the Breton saints, as we have seen, and Saxon raids were not unknown during the uncertain times after the departure of the Romans, although usually nearer to the coast than a place like Lanrivoaré. For some, this was more likely the work of a band of marauding Viking raiders of the 9th century, and they certainly did get about in Brittany at that time. Christianity would surely have had potential enemies in these early stages, even if the culprits can't be pinned down. That much of the legend is not hard to appreciate. A change of religion is, after all, one of the biggest transformations of them all, and one which could lead to challenge and death on this earth. The story poses immediate practical problems, however, with the space not in any way big enough to hold the remains of such huge numbers. That's if it was even feasible that a community of so great a size existed anywhere near here in those times. The current population of Lanviroaré is about 1500, just for a fun comparison, because the numbers game is part of the undoubted charm of this unconventional place.

Traditionally the cemetery's name refers to the very specific number of 7777 saints, a forcefully sacred figure on the basis of seven's eternal religiosity, and even more powerful by such compelling repetition (just imagine 7777 deadly sins), but that calculation apparently springs from a mistranslation of a Breton saying on the matter:

Seiz mil, seiz kant, seiz ugent ha seiz
A zo beziet e Gouled Breiz

This does not mean seven thousand, seven hundred and seventy-seven at all, although you can see how without a good knowledge of Breton, one could make the assumption, but rather:

Seven thousand, seven hundred and twenty times seven plus seven
Are buried in Basse Bretagne

This actually gives us a total of 7847. It doesn't quite have the same stature as a number somehow. And then for some reason that escapes my true understanding, although it has something to do with Druid calculations of the surface area of a circle of 100m in diameter, we are to add the stone loaves, and end up with a grand total of 7854 and have nowhere further to go. Something of a mystery there, but some point out the possible derivation at the origin of all this mathematical calculation from the traditional anecdote concerning *sex milia, sexcenti, sexaginta sex* (6666) warriors, mentioned in the Latin text of a 12th century Life of Saint Goëznou. It's not difficult to see how one could have slipped into the other on a surface reading. The reference is to this traditional number of a Roman legion as still existing in the saint's time in a Breton town called Legione (possibly what is today Brest, which is not a million miles from Lanrivoaré). So maybe the soldiers got confused with (or transformed into?) a very large number of Christian martyrs in the volatile world of legend. It's all a bit spooky, however you do the numbers.

To return to what lies on or in the ground at Lanrivoaré: as a focus of faith and martyrdom on such a scale, it not surprisingly became a place of pilgrimage. All the victims of whatever happened were saints by popular acclaim and in the more traditional sense of dying for their religion. The intense sanctity conferred by such numbers brought a compelling cachet of healing potential, and many came to this holy spot in the hope of cures. According to an old custom, it was only acceptable to touch the sacred ground on one's knees or with bare feet (bare head goes without saying) and those disrespecting this would be punished by illness. Mothers who came here to pray for their children to walk strongly, apparently a special gift of the place, were to go seven times around the perimeter stones. Fortunately not 7777 times. A salutary tale is told of someone disrespecting the custom and keeping his shoes on, then being struck down by a strange malady. I didn't know about all this until after leaving the precinct in my walking boots and rain-hat...

Dancing maidens, barking dogs, loaves of bread all solidified in the name of Christian values. It's a rather less positive picture than the thought of standing-stones being a representation of the ancestors, symbolically mutated from one substance to another, making lasting memory. But with all these varied changes comes the energy of renewal and the chance for later generations and different peoples to bring their own perspectives to old tales, or indeed to invent others. Let's go back to that wedding party group on the dark heath in the Monts d'Arrée, now, for their flippant disregard of the priest, nothing more than a gently curving line of 77 (no!) stones. What if – and this is only idle speculation – those revellers were not really men but had actually been stones originally, sucked out of their tough quartz-speckled skin into the more fluid world of humans by the curse of a witch. They might then be quite content to be back in their natural lithic state, making the joke on the priest this time round. There's a new story there in the making…

The most important lesson of transformation is that things don't stay the same. And for that we should be grateful.

10 Performance

Some stones have to entertain to earn their identity. Certain ones are said to be active in their own right, and others have special qualities that induce performance in collusion with humans. People believed (and still believe in some cases) that interaction with these latter stones could bring benefits such as providing answers to questions or offering healing. Direct touch, creating an intimacy of connection, becomes the catalyst for a positive result. Expectations were created as tales passed from person to person, and some individual rocks became famous for their powers, entering the cultural legacy of their communes. We have already seen the common popular view that some menhirs move, whether this is turning on the spot or heading off for a midnight bathe in the ocean. The crucial detail is that the movement is one of extreme rapidity, so fast that it defeats human comprehension, a journey of miles accomplished in the time it takes the clock to strike. A cynic might jeer at this notion, but some people sincerely believed that there were stones that shifted themselves from one spot to another.

Sound, in relation to megaliths, has begun to be considered as a possible factor in the original concept of neolithic monuments, and the naturally musical properties of certain minerals is nowhere better illustrated than in the **Pierres sonnantes** (Ringing Stones) in the Arguenon estuary near Créhen. They have a fine location on the tidal shore, overlooked by the haunting ruins of the Château du Guildo (see Chapter 8) across the water. My first encounter was with a group of low dark blocks wedged in the sand close to the bank and accessible along the river edge at low tide. Paul Sébillot's 1880s description of 'a troop of crouching black sheep' seemed something of an exaggeration, until I learnt later that the main conglomeration of ringing stones lay well round the bend in the river. I had not gone far enough to get the full effect. A second visit revealed the true extent of the phenomenon, which is indeed impressive, with many sizeable examples, and I went from one to another, tapping at the (indicated) right place to extricate a metallic ring.

Pierres sonnantes

A large semi-suspended stone right under the arched bank was helpfully pointed out by a local dog-walker as emitting the best sound. It did indeed give an intensely satisfying resonance, like flicking crystal glass with the fingers. But each rock produced a slightly different note and it might have been interesting to try out harmonies with a group of people. To get the full musical effect you need to strike the sweet spot on one of the ringers with another stone of the same dense type. These dark rocks are dolerite, a bit like basalt, an exceptionally hard igneous stone which can scratch glass. There is no sign of any others in the area except for this belt of ringing stones on the beach. It is easy to see that iron constitutes a large part of their make-up and it is this mineral composition that produces the effects. Helped doubtless by their legendary origins in the pit of Gargantua's stomach, as we are also told that the giant spewed them up after a surfeit of scallops from the estuary waters. The Ringing Stones have been a tourist attraction for getting on for 150 years, and at the beginning of 20th century, early postcards portray visitors led to the scene by local children, and doubtless shown 'how to do it'. Thus the stones and the children both perform for a captive audience, who are then invited up onto the stage to have a go themselves.

Rocks that rock are fairly common in Brittany. These are large, imposing boulders delicately balanced on the ground or another stone, which can be set in gentle motion if touched in the right way in the right place. No force should be needed, although frustration does lead to over-enthusiastic effort sometimes. It is an edifying spectacle to sit for an hour and watch how people prepare for and then try to carry out the endeavour. And how they respond to success or the more usual failure afterwards. In the summer tourist season with a large crowd gathered, it takes on the guise of a genuine spectator sport. But attempting the challenge puts oneself into a long timeline of the community of stone-rockers, and gives a gratifying sense of shared achievement. These shaking stones are usually known as *branlante* (wobbly) or sometimes *tremblante* (trembling). Jacques Cambry in a text of the last years of the 18th century mentions interest in this phenomenon, so the practice goes back for hundreds of years. Some early antiquarians of the 19th century thought they were crafted in this way by human hand, but they are natural rocks, often exposed and destabilised at a fairly late stage of their existence by the removal of others around them.

From stimulating casual curiosity, some have morphed into vigorous heritage symbols, giving definition, and occasionally notoriety, to their location, and attracting numerous visitors. Their unusual natural qualities also give rise to legends (or not, in one famous case) which add to the attraction. And their interactive element is a special draw for the curious: there is appeal in a sort of game with such ancient and unpromising material, even if it might be going a bit far to speak of a heroic task on a par with lifting the sword from the stone. To this day, passing locals often play a part in initiation for less fortunate outsiders, but it used to be common for youngsters of the parish to hang around offering to reveal the secret in return for a small tip, the *petits guides* mentioned above, and active at many sites.

There could hardly be a greater contrast between the **Roche tremblante (Trembling Rock)** in Huelgoat forest and the **Men Dogan (Cuckolds' Stone)** in Trégunc. One has a strong history of popular importance as a divinatory tool, the other doesn't even have a legend to call its own. Which do you think is venerated and promoted today? Sadly, you're wrong. The Trembling Rock with its forest setting is the best known of these movers and shakers, despite the more impressive pedigree of the other. It is a massive stone, weighing an estimated 137 tons, poised on a narrow ledge on a steep hillside near the Chaos. Below there's a modern structure housing a crêperie on what was the site of the manager's offices when the whole area was a quarry. The local granite, an often large-grained grey to grey-blue, is a highly sought-after building stone, which has been used in the construction of many churches and chapels as well as things like canal locks and viaducts. This particular area, the Bois du Saoulec, was heavily exploited in the 19th century.

The Trembling Rock itself bears a line of chisel holes making it ready for splitting, an indication of how close this stone came to figuring in the last chapter of this book. With survival, it has become one of the most sought-after sights in the forest, with

La Roche tremblante

queues forming at busy times, arguments breaking out over whether the wretched thing has moved or not, and rare bursts of applause marking success. Old people of the village today recall that young people learnt to manipulate the stone in a kind of rite of passage. Being able to do it, even today, is a mark of prowess, although the whole thing has become a stage for performance art, with crowds of tourists huffing and puffing in the attempt, and an occasional local deigning to rock the huge stone with the lightest of touches at the perfect spot. I remember a very kind old man moving the stone from the opposite side to the claimed optimal pressure point whilst allowing a child to be filmed by his mother with his little back bent under the rock, apparently responsible for the rocking motion.

But the Trembling Rock, thanks to its late exposure on the scene in this magical forest, has no established legend of fairies or korrigans or even those mad old giants from the nearby Chaos. (A fate it shares with the Mushroom nearby, another stone revealed by quarrying activity.) A famous stone without a story, now there's a rarity. There have of course been recent attempts to create some (it shivers with appreciation of tourist acclaim…) and give better context for this performing monster, but the lack of success perhaps indicates that the time for the creation of traditional type stories is gone and we must move to new ideas, maybe tales based on earth energies or AI or the type of 'treasure' sought for in GPS caching to provide a meaningful new life for this particular stone. On the other hand, who needs this hype when the stone rocks? That *is* the story.

However, the **Men Dogan** or the *Pierre des cocus* at Kerouel in Trégunc does more. It is, or was, a rocking stone with real value-added, taking a role in the domestic life of humans, through its movements offering answers to questions posed. In the 19th century some antiquarians made this claim for it as a divinatory stone in general terms. According to the Chevalier du Freminville, who naturally saw it in the context of Druid practices, its oscillations would be interpreted by a priest to give some specific response to a particular question. So perhaps the pedigree of replying to demand is genuinely a long one, even if the subject matter came to be much more specific as time went on. The stone is said to be extremely sensitive to touch, capable of being moved with a single finger correctly placed, this facility perhaps taken into account in the way questions were asked. But whilst humans made the decision to seek a resolution of their anxieties, the stone's own power was thought to be enshrined in the process and decisive in the result. It could respond or withhold an affirmation: it was the arbiter of truth.

This rock's famous speciality was fidelity. The name means Cuckold's Stone, and in popular tradition it was where husbands would come to find out if their wives were faithful. In that case, the man would be able to rock the stone. It is said that this was a first port of call for sailors returning from long trips at sea. If it didn't move, suspicions were well-founded, and let's face it, mainly suspicious husbands would be the ones to carry out the ritual in the first place. (One hopes women had their own stone somewhere nearby.) The great literary lion Flaubert came to see the Men Dogan during his tour of Brittany in 1847, having apparently heard of its reputation back in Paris! He tried to move it, but the rock was unresponsive. '*Ça ne fait rie*n,' he said dismissively. '*Je suis célibataire.*' So what? I'm a bachelor anyway. His subsequent mention of the stone in the account of his travels gave it an even greater notoriety and increased the number of tourists visiting the site.

This plump plum of a rock, a mighty stone once consulted by many and visited out of respect for its reputation by others, is now a sad sight. Unsigned, under-valued and totally neglected. Although it can be seen just metres away from the busy D783 between Trégunc and Concarneau, it is not easy to access, as surrounded by worked fields, and the tiny outcrop where it sits raised above ground level, is almost completely obscured by prickly gorse and brambles. A local who lives nearby was very surprised I could be bothered. With effort and a few scratches, it is possible to get within touching distance, but it is impractical to stand back and get a good view with the pressing vegetation all around. The boulder, balanced on a ledge of exposed rock, is 3.7 x 2.70m of rounded granite, weighing more than 50 tons. Ivy trails down the sides and little shards of bark seem to grow on one face as if it was a tree in another life. I have to say it remained disappointingly unmoved by my visit.

The Men Dogan plays a crucial part in the mawkish melodrama of Mao and Corentine, a story told in 1867 by collector of Breton legends, Ernest du Laurens de la Barre, a *notaire* from Quimper.

Mao, a poor young man, fell deeply in love with the beautiful Corentine, ward of a prosperous uncle who would give her a good dowry. He used to follow her about, gazing longingly, and so became known to her. But because she was such a sought-after prize, he had little likelihood of success in his pursuit and decided to consult a tailor reputed to have magical powers. This man fancied his own chances at Corentine's hand and saw an opportunity to get rid of a rival. He advised Mao to go at midnight to consult the Men Dogan. He must try three times to make the stone move, and if it did, that meant the girl would not love him. (In other words, the tailor tricked him, as this was the reverse of how the stone actually operated, with movement indicating a positive answer.) The young man was ready to try anything, and walked across the countryside through the darkness into the looming presence of the great rock. He made a first attempt. Nothing happened. A second. Still no movement. He began to hope. Third time, the stone rocked. Mao despaired at this answer and stumbled away over the rough fields to the shore. Overwhelmed by hopelessness in the face of life without his love, he drowned himself in the sea. When Corentine heard the news she was devastated, having secretly favoured him all along. The tragedy caused her to lose her mind, and she used to sit on top of the Men Dogan singing sadly and saying aloud: 'Mao is not dead. He is under the rock. I'm waiting for Jesus to give me the strength to lift it.'

In 1882, not long after the publication of this pitiful story, the Men Dogan survived destruction after a campaign by local worthies, and was classified as an Historic Monument in that year. A postcard from c1900 labels the stone *Pierre tremblante de la fidelité* (trembling rock of fidelity). The early photo shows two boys perched on top of the rock and four girls on the ground below. Clearly the stone had already made its mark in tourism. The combination of children in traditional Breton costume and a mysterious moving rock that could provide answers about the state of your marriage was not surprisingly a big draw. Local children hung around to demonstrate the movement to visitors and pocket a reward in return. It is said that the rock was blocked with a small pebble if the money was not up front...

Often megalithic sites are associated with fertility and hopes of marriage, interacting in the ordinary life of ordinary people in a way the Church could not condone. The power of superstition and tradition in this sense has always been strong in Brittany and is clearly still in action today, as we have seen. Natural rocks also seem to make their mark in this context. One out-of-the-way place almost on the Normandy border is the energetically powerful **Buttes de Monthault**, a treasure store of sacred stones. This distinctive wooded hill gave its name ('high mountain') to the village a kilometre away. It is littered with mossy boulders, and supports on the summit, framed by evergreens, a neo-Gothic chapel of 1877, dedicated to Notre-Dame de la Délivrance, last in a long series of religious buildings on this spot. There is also a range of modern sculptures, featuring Celtic patterns and a huge hand. On a day with few visitors, especially early in the morning, it has a real sense of a place apart, full of present spirits.

Four special ancient rocks ranged across the hillside form the real mythology of the place and create a sense of magic and mystery. **La pierre au sacrifice** (sacrificial stone) is from the common tradition of attribution to Druid rituals, a flattish surface with a large depression where, imaginatively, blood pooled and then drained away. (It may actually have been used for the same death ritual mentioned below at Mane Guen.) **La pierre au diable** (Devil's stone) still bears the marks of his claws before Satan dropped it here rather carelessly during the building of Mont-Saint-Michel, only 35 kilometres away. **La pierre aux moines** (Monks' stone), was the name given to the largest (rocking) stone of a natural structure looking remarkably like a neolithic dolmen or at least the home of a family of korrigans. It was the legendary dwelling of a hermit, but the one we actually know of, Jean Guenée, lived in a cabin beside it up until the time of the Revolution, welcoming pilgrims travelling to or from the Abbey of Mont-Saint-Michel.

Most notable of all the stones here is **La Roche écrianté,** a Gallo word for *glissante* or slippery. It is a huge mass of rock (13m x 5m) with a deep gash beside the shiny vertical line of wear giving a hint of the old custom. Here the performance requires rock and human in harmony. The idea was for girls to slide down (preferably *à cul nu* or bare-assed), and then to leave a tribute to the rock of a small piece of cloth or ribbon. After carrying out this rite, they could be sure of getting married within the year. Early postcards of the rock stick mainly to the safer illustration of little boys tobogganing down. But photos do not show the view from the top downwards. In reality, it is a shock to see that the rock is very steep indeed and the descent could have been quite scary, lending it even more significance as a ritual. A trial of courage!

The accumulation of these associations in one place suggests a long spiritual heritage for the site of Monthault. At the very least it is a beautiful natural refuge from the outside world in turbulent times. Walking up from the village adds the important notion of journey to prepare for arrival on the hill, creating a sense of anticipation for the presence of the stones. Even now, the progression from sacred rock to sacred rock is a form of soothing ritual, giving the feeling of participation in something ancient and valued over time by great numbers of people. The acknowledgement of the stones and their stories is the way for us to contribute to this heritage and take it forward for the future. In return we share, in our brief moment, their calm grey eternity.

Agency in the fulfilment of vows was an important role for many stones which attracted the devotion and loyalty of locals over centuries. The offerings and messages left today in the hope that desires will be granted are continuing a timeless belief in the practice of reciprocation, a formula in which the stone had a crucial part to play. We have already seen imaginatively potent locations like Merlin's tomb attracting fervent written prayers and gifts in the hope of fulfilment of vows. Stones associated with saints also became the focus of many such rituals. One of the most moving, in its hidden simplicity, is the cult of **Saint Nonne and her sacred rocks** in Dirinon, Finistère. Nonne came to Brittany in the late 5th century as a pregnant refugee, after being raped by the Welsh king Ceredig. She arrived at this secret place in the forest of Landerneau to give birth to her child.

The pretty *fontaine* dedicated to Nonne and still containing a statue of the saint reading a book, is beside a little road, but visitors are often unaware that tucked away in the woods nearby is a weathered block of stone, nearly two metres long, with ten cupules, said to show the imprint of her knees as she prayed for a safe birth.

It is covered not only in lichen but in offerings to this day, maintaining a long custom. Small stones, crosses made from twigs and even simple gifts of leaves and wild plants are always to be seen lying here, evidence of continued belief in the heavenly aid of saints. It is known locally as a *pierre à voeux* or wishing stone, a place where the saint's help is called on in many situations, often connected with childbirth and children because of her own story. This feels like a special, hopeful sort of place, out of the ordinary, not for everyone to find, and again it is a place where the magic lies in the stone itself, even if it is thought to have taken on special energies from the circumstances of Nonne's situation.

Another stone beside the *fontaine*, whose waters were reputed to cure eye problems, is called the Cradle of Divy (David, Dewi), where the saint is said to have given birth to her son, who would one day become the patron saint of Wales. The 16th century *Life of Saint Nonne* describes her amazement when the 'opportune' stone opened up under the pressure of her hands to make a dip in the middle. The block of quartzite, according to Hippolyte Sarton, a late 19th century traveller, 'softened like wax' to form the cradle to receive the baby, after he had been washed in the water of the source. This stone is also regarded as a wishing stone by some today, and is much better known thanks to its proximity to the walls around the source.

All this is well out of the *bourg* of Dirinon, whose name means 'the oak trees of Nonne'. Here the saint has an impressive church dating from the late 16th century, topped by an attractive galleried bell-tower, and Nonne's tomb with a recumbent statue on the sarcophagus. A chapel is also contained within the precinct and this building has an unusual block of schist protruding high up from the exterior wall. Apparently, the first attempts to erect this place of worship for the saint's memory took place elsewhere, but each night the work of the day was mysteriously destroyed. Finally the architect deduced that the saint herself wanted a say. He had a large stone placed on an ox cart and let the animals go where they would. This is the spot where they stopped, and the special stone was incorporated in a rather striking fashion in the construction to commemorate this marvel.

From help at the beginning of a human life, what could be more important than the same at the end, a smoothing and securing of the passage from worldly existence to death? When old people were lingering without actually dying, there was a saying *mal e in cas de Lomeltrow* or 'time to send them to **Locmeltro**'. This small village not far from Guern contains the **Chapelle de Saint Meldéoc**, inside which is a very curious stone. It is known as the **mell beniguet**, although this name is not without its difficulty, with *mel* and *mell* meaning mallet and ball respectively. *Beniguet* is unequivocally 'blessed'. (Some even prefer to see a distortion of *men beniguet* – blessed stone.) The stone concerned at Locmeltro is indeed a big round ball, but given the association of Ankou, the Grim Reaper, with a *maillet*, this seems the obvious interpretation, because it is in effect an instrument of death. In the *Barzaz Breiz*, that seminal collection of Breton ballads published in 1839 by Theodore de la Villemarqué, there is a reference to this accoutrement: 'I hear the blows of the little hammer of Ankou (as a soul leaves the body)'. The purpose of the *mell beniguet* is to release the soul and free the spirit of the dying. It was said, for example, that at Quelven there was a blessed stone, a kind of stone ball, that was placed on the head of a dying person to shorten their agony.

It may have become a purely symbolic act, the stone put carefully on the forehead or the pillow, psychologically important to the sufferer who has requested it, as a sign that departure from life will now come swiftly. This appears to be how the rite developed in the 20th century. But earlier, tapping the head with the implement was probably the essence of the practice, which may go back to ancient times, a distant relative of the opening of the 7th (crown) chakra to release the spirit in Hinduism. The first mention of the Breton tradition came in 1847. According to François-Marie Cayot-Délandre in his *Guide du Morbihan*, old people used to go to the summit of Mane Guen, one of the seven sacred hills of Brittany, and have a Druid finish them off by striking their heads with a sacred mallet. This custom later was to be brought into the fold of the Church, seen as a humanitarian gesture to bring peace to sufferers and offer an easier passage into death. The task was given to the oldest member of the community when asked for by a dying person, and while the verger said a prayer and the bell was rung, the *mell beniguet* was used to relieve the sufferer of his or her final agonies.

Paul Aveneau de la Grancière in *Traditions et légendes au pays d'Armor* (1900) wrote of a famous *massue bénie* or mallet used to strike down old people who were taking a long time to die or suffering terribly. He called it *mael beniget*. In 1903, a condescending response by Joseph Loth retorted that *mell* (not *mael*) meant ball, citing the example of *jouer à la soule* (to play a traditional ball game) being *mellat* in Breton. He also defines the place-name Locmeltro as 'sacred place (*loc*) in the valley (*trou*) of the ball (*mell*)'. But a ball-shaped stone can be a mallet in function if not appearance, as subsequent commentators generally accepted. These blessed stones were well-known in the diocese of Vannes and kept in various chapels. In 1909 Zacharie de Rouzic attested that at Saint-Guenin there were two (balls of dark blue schist), which had been used to break many skulls.

The *mell beniguet* in Locmeltro is a large granite ball of 3kg, 42cm in circumference, and with a reddish tinge. Another glowing red stone! The chapel only seems to be open during the summer festival of *Art dans les chapelles* and it took me several goes to get access. I have to say, however, that I found this stone completely mesmerising, not only from morbid fascination about what it had seen and done, but its intrinsic qualities. It may not be the only one of its kind, but it felt unique to me and I had real difficulty in finally tearing myself away. Primitive and other-worldly, like an object from space, it is set in a glass case, so it resembles the moon, suspended in its own mini-universe. It definitely has the potential of a cult object in its own right, such is the sense of contained potency. Once the initial awe had subsided a little, I couldn't help the unworthy thought that the line between tapping and bashing may sometimes have been crossed in the interest of rapid inheritance. It's a formidable object to employ in contact with a fragile old skull, especially if left overnight in the presence of unscrupulous relatives.

This whole place at Locmeltro is intriguing. The low chapel is set in an open valley location, once part of the park of the local château, with the *fontaine* a little distance away across a wide grassy space, beside a large bread oven. The site was in ruins in the 1950s and much work has been carried out to restore the building and re-establish the annual Pardon. The identity of the saint is a little vague. Meldéoc was a 7th century Bishop of Vannes, but some suggest Mélar as an alternative. In the precinct itself is a free-standing bell 'tower', two wooden posts and a slated roof like a hat, low enough for anyone to reach the rope. There are three Iron Age steles (or perhaps one and two halves), including a stoup that may be a scooped out Roman borne. Opposite the chapel sit a calvary and a line of what look like ancient graves, the whole creating one of those irresistible places where the elements add up to a rich atmosphere of history and stone secrets. It would make an excellent setting for drama.

How important are all these stones that provide humans with entertainment or services, from conjuring up pleasant musical sound to bopping dying people on the head. These interactions are at the heart of what many esteem in stones today, a little challenge and a sense of their long-standing role in the life of a community. This latter aspect offers us the cohesive value of shared experience – not only with people, but with the stones themselves.

11 Memorial

Memorials can have many functions. They may be reminders, statements of belief, tokens of respect, articulation of the communal pain of mourning, evidence of pride, warnings to be derived from tragedy. Ultimately, they stand up for the past, a cogent stage in the line of action and interpretation. Brittany is full of memorials celebrating life and honouring death, fitting for a place where ancestors are ever present and the close relation between past and present is perpetuated in popular tradition. Stones are bound up with memory: lasting, monumental and representative of fundamental ties with the earth, our connection to long history. They plug a gap in the unknown. The incorporation of megaliths into some war memorials ties the remote past of Brittany to the modern world, and brings us into direct affiliation with our most distant forebears, for we all belong together and the link of stone naturally expresses this on-going reality.

The well-kept graveyards of Brittany reflect the strong continuing tradition of death as part of life, with families assiduously tending their plots, especially at Toussaint or All Saints at the end of October, when the dead come into their own and welcome a pot or two of chrysanthemums. But it's more than domestic pride or social custom. The dead live on as long as they are remembered. The oral tradition preserves a fine canon of stories figuring the character of death, which has always provided a lively flirtation for the Bretons. **Ankou**, the skeletal Grim Reaper, appears in sculpted form on many a religious building as a reminder to the living arriving for church services that they are all ultimately entering his territory. He is the sequel to daily activity and no-one will escape his fatal visit.

Lannédern has a particularly fine example, a weird combination

Ankou, Lannédern

of charm and menace, in its exquisite little parish close, complete with views to the summits of the Monts d'Arrée. The skeleton, an edging detail on the exterior of a south facing window, seems to be sitting on the roof, grinning, bearing an arrow, with an indecipherable slogan below. Opposite is a figure harder to define, a different form of Ankou perhaps, seen by some as an angelic psychopomp, another function of this harbinger of death. The little ossuary building in Renaissance style from the 1660s nearby is complete with symbolic skulls and crossbones, plus an angelic banner bearing the words COGITA MORI (think about what's in store) mirrored on the opposite corner by RESPICE FINEM, which amounts to the same thing. You might almost call this whole ensemble of mortuary emblems an anticipatory memorial.

The figure with a similar weapon on the charnel house at **La Roche Maurice** is more pragmatic and bears the blunt boast: *je vous tue tous*, I kill you all. This prompt about the levelling factor of Ankou's activity must have been of strange comfort to many poorer members of society. It comes to the same for everyone in the end. This idea is memorably visualised in the rare surviving Dance of Death murals, with earliest Breton example (fragmentary) at Kernascléden in Morbihan and most graphically of all at the chapel Kermaria-an-Iskuit in Plouha, where the late 15th century *danse macabre* lights up the arches above the nave with an emperor, king, bishop, nobles and many professional people led by Ankou's helpers to their doom along with the *hoi polloi*. Is it a story about life or death?

Memorials differ from objective historical accounts (if such things exist) in that they openly represent the views of a particular group or even an individual. They may be selective with facts or concerned only with one aspect of an event. History is invariably more complex than a single memorial can convey. Monuments are often indelibly linked to a sense of place, like the record of some specific happenings considered below, or more generally representative, or both, like the modern **Mémorial de l'Abolition d'Esclavage** (the abolition of the slave trade). This unforgettable historical landmark opened on the Quai de la Fosse in **Nantes** in 2012 after many years of preparation, fittingly for a city which was a major point of departure for the 'triangular trade', taking goods to Africa, slaves to the West Indies and then tropical goods back to Brittany. It takes the form of a huge structure of stone – using blocks from the original quays – wood, concrete and glass, with an effect both gleaming and stark, leading down symbolically on a path of uncomfortable memory to the underground section, presented unemotionally, like the architecture. Here a vast plate of glass is inscribed with texts on the subject of abolition, and on the pavements above, alongside the Loire, 2000 little glass inserts give the name and date of each ship that came and went with its terrible cargo, as well as the ports concerned. Less is more in this case, often so for intensity of feeling. The memorial has only to act as a trigger, it does not need to provide forensic detail, it's a state of mind not a state of being, for memory is not the same as history, although both are subject to re-interpretation over time.

The past still looms large in the constant equation of Breton identity, with historical events that forged this chimera frequently recorded in memorials set in stone. These enshrine what certain groups of people want to remember and how they want to remember it. Simplification of convoluted narrative is inevitable, but may also be deliberately selective, where a decent historical account would not be able to ignore two sides of a dispute. Events in history contributing to the construction of Bretons' sense of pride and patriotic beliefs have their lasting traces on the ground in the form of statues, plaques and monuments. They present the heroic struggle of Brittany against foreign enemies (Franks, English, French, Germans) and record key moments in the development of the Breton state.

Its origins in the 9th century with a communal rallying against Frankish imperialism are commemorated in **Bains-sur-Oust** by a glum stylised 1952 **statue of leader Nominoë**, whose glorious career kick-started Brittany's own period of political expansion. This Count of Poher (or Vannes) selected by the Emperor of the Franks Louis Le Pieux as a suitably stabilising leader for the troublesome Bretons, was game-keeper turned poacher when Charles the Bald succeeded to the throne in Paris in 843. Nominoë quickly seized his opportunity to take the offensive against the Franks, seeing off these heavy-armed opponents at Ballon (845), where a hamlet called La Bataille has an old memorial cross. A contemporary art installation (2018) commemorating the battle is a more grandiose and original reminder today.

This clash may not have been the decisive engagement later claimed, but confused by 19th century historians with a major battle fought by the Breton leader's son in 851. In terms of the mythology of Brittany's origins, however, the event at Ballon remains seminal regardless. In nearby Bains-sur-Oust, the emblematic granite statue of Nominoë is by Raffig Tullou, prominent neo-Druid and a member of the Seiz Breur movement, particularly active between the two World Wars, aimed at revitalising Breton art and culture with a new style fused from traditional and contemporary motifs. The glorification of this victory over the future French is an important part of the modern Breton nationalism narrative. It encourages some to elevate Nominoë to the status of first King of Brittany, which is a dubious claim – he is usually styled *duc / dux* (leader) in the documentary sources, although his son Erispoë was genuinely crowned. Nominoë, however, remains a refreshingly energetic figure, with a dynamism not at all conveyed by the heavy statue, and it is not surprising that his thrusting confidence endures as the signal example of Breton potential later squeezed and desiccated by French overlordship.

At **Mi-voie between Josselin and Ploërmel** close to the RN24 stands a granite column of 30 stones (**Colonne des Trente**) commemorating the Combat of the Thirty on 26th or 27th March in 1351. This took place on a fixed field of battle in the shade of a great oak tree, a detail faithfully portrayed in the famous 1857 painting of that fateful day by Octave Penguilly L'Haridon, whose depiction of the battle was commissioned by Napoléon III. The

30-a-side engagement was carried out in the context of the Hundred Years War between England and France, and it is often presented as a match between Bretons and the English. This would always be a simplistic view of the situation in Brittany at that time, when the real conflict was between rival claimants to the dukedom: Jean III had died in 1541 without an heir and his position was claimed by his niece Jeanne de Penthièvre (in the person of her husband, Charles de Blois) and Jean de Montfort, half-brother of the duke. The War of Succession which ensued was a long drawn-out, bloody affair, with the French (under King Philip VI de Valois) supporting Charles de Blois, and the Montforts enjoying English backing from Edward III. The great families of Brittany chose their side with an eye to future favour, which muddies the waters of the Breton v English claims in 1351. The 'English' side included at least four Bretons and six German mercenaries.

The combat was a pre-arranged stylised affair between the rival garrisons at Ploërmel (led by Englishman Bembro or Bembrough) and Josselin (led by Breton Jean de Beaumanoir) to settle a question of honour, as the Breton commander had made a complaint about the English soldiers' poor treatment of local inhabitants. A few months earlier, the English nobleman Thomas Dagworth had been ambushed and killed near Auray in a perceived violation of an armistice. Bembrough seems to have taken a sort of revenge in the countryside around Ploërmel, his English soldiers raping and murdering with impunity, and the peasants chained like slaves. But he refuted his opponent's claims of oppression, and the proposal to fight it out at an agreed time and place soon followed.

Early in the morning on the day, Beaumanoir, partisan of Charles de Blois, attended the church in Josselin for mass, confession and absolution, before proceeding to Mi-Voie with his companions. The religious devotions of the Bretons made them later to the scene than their opponents. The opening to the *Barzaz*

Breiz's dramatic account sets the scene: after commenting on the appalling weather of that March, the conclusion is drawn – 'worse than the winds and the rain are the detestable English!' It goes on to give the Bretons' prayer to Saint Cado (see p.112) before the contest began, and they then came face to face with Robert Bembrough, leader of the Montfortists, and his own thirty men. The painting mentioned above unflinchingly summons up the raw brutality of what was in effect a contest between heavily-armed individuals on foot, with no scope for escape from the constant impetus of attack and defence.

The fighting began at 11 o'clock and the initial clash was fast and furious. Two on each side were quickly killed and after a break for wounds to be treated, Bembrough himself fell in the melee, leaving the English temporarily in disarray. But they rallied in 'hedgehog' formation and the battle continued. The most famous anecdote of the whole affair is recorded in the *Chronicles* of Froissart, a contemporary. It concerns Beaumanoir, who was fasting on the day, and, having been wounded, called for a drink to keep up his strength. One of his companions, Geffroy du Bois retorted: 'Drink your blood, Beaumanoir, that'll quench your thirst.' In the poem about this event in the *Barzaz Breiz*, a young equerry keeps tally, like a refrain, enumerating those involved, then the number of mounting dead. By the end of the day, this included 12-17 on the English side and 6 on the Breton. Not a single fighter remained untouched. Many years later Froissart actually met one of the battle-scarred survivors, Even (Yves) Charruel. The leaderless English were finally broken and surrendered. Beaumanoir victoriously led his Breton troops and English prisoners back to Josselin, their helmets decorated with sprigs of broom from the field of battle.

The mythology of this event has grown with time. In 1351 it was of no real significance, a small local event, more like a particularly bloody tournament than an engagement of strategic importance. The way in which it has been remembered is what has done the trick and this involved the establishment of the granite memorial at Mi-Voie between 1819 and 1823. (An older cross of commemoration, renewed after destruction in the Revolution, is situated behind the monument.) This was under the continuing influence of Chouannerie in the area, regarded by many as a Breton movement against the imposition of the new Republic by the French. The Chouans were devout Catholic monarchists, opposed to the outcome of the Revolution, which ended the special privileges of Brittany's own government and attacked the religious faith that was at the heart of Breton culture. The monument at Mi-Voie was a blow struck for Breton tradition and resistance to imposition.

The obelisk 'to the glory of the thirty Bretons' stands 13m high, made up of regular granite blocks. On one side the names of Beaumanoir's companions are recorded, but there is no mention of the other participants. The inaugural plaque tellingly begins VIVE LE ROI, LES BOURBONS TOUJOURS (Long live the king! Bourbons forever), making the motivation for this edifice clear, and further on the inscription urges the Breton posterity to 'Imitate your ancestors'. The anti-English image of the commemoration would also have echoes later in the 19th century with the resentment of imperialism (French and English) and growing Celtic awareness. It was to become a renewed focus of patriotism with the resurgence of Breton nationalism and intense emphasis on Breton pride in the past. The URB (Union régionaliste bretonne), an important organisation with primarily cultural aims, fostering interest in folklore and traditional customs, was founded in 1898. So the obelisk remains, dedicated 'To the perpetual memory of the battle of the Thirty', and the memory will certainly last as long as the column stands...

The powerful symbolism of place in memorial is nowhere more evident than **Saint-Aubin-du-Cormier**, in the Marches of Brittany, the borderlands so constantly fought over by Breton and Franks/French. At the battle here in 1488 (see p.133), any realistic prospect of Breton autonomy came to an end, even though there were to be years of intricate political tussle before the irrevocable loss of independence and the arrival of unequivocal French domination in 1532. The area has always been of historical and legendary interest, but early 20th century patriotic movements saw the politicisation which has made the site of the battle a *haut lieu* of Breton nationalism. The low **Monument aux Bretons** stands by the main road to Sens-de-Bretagne, bearing the ducal blazon of ermines and surmounted by a military cross *pattée*, and a more secret earlier memorial is concealed on the moor in the Bois d'Uzel nearby.

Marking memory by celebrating anniversaries with ceremonies and monuments is a key factor in perpetuating what is believed about the past. Here the main monument was erected in 1988 for the 500th anniversary of the battle by the association Souvenir Breton, whilst the older one is a much earlier tribute, put up in 1932 by the Parti national breton (the Breton nationalist party). The conflict saw 10-12,000 men in the army of Duke François II, and 15,000 on the French side, which included Bretons, commanded by Louis de la Trémoille. The 1988 memorial pays tribute to those who fell fighting to defend Breton liberty in the army of the duke, with each section having their own plaque: 6,000 Bretons, 3500 Spanish, Gascons, Basques, 800 Germans and 500 English volunteer archers (under the command of one Talbot). Acknowledgement here extends to all who took up arms against the power of France. The relatively light losses on the French side are not recorded.

The area is now called **La Lande de la Rencontre**, recording that fatal encounter. Last time I went to this site a few years ago, a tiny unmarked path led from a track through overgrown vegetation in the Bois d'Uzel to an outcrop of rock with a stumpy cross and a plaque bearing the simple message in Breton 'The French beat the Bretons, 28th July 1488. Let us not forget!' and in French '6000 Bretons died here defending Breton independence', with the date. Note the difference between the two versions. The simplicity of this sobering record and heartfelt exhortation is stirring, and the natural setting contributes a deep spirit of place to the memory of this crucial event in Breton history. It's a moving memorial, unlike the rather chill ugly monument by the main road. Perhaps it is too much to ask of one stone monument and a few epigraphs to reproduce the energy and passion of the original struggle in this historic landscape.

These days there is also a sculpture park in the process of development by MAB (Musée Archipel Breton), featuring the grumpy-faced head and shoulders of Anne de Bretagne popping out of a volcano shaped stone, and a new more vibrant representation of Nominoë, inaugurated in 2021. This association emerged from another battle here in the early 21st century, coming together to stop this significant terrain where the historic event took place – and where the remains of thousands still lie – being turned into a repository for household waste. They have purchased a parcel of land with the long-term intention of founding a museum to the memory of the military loss that so significantly marked a changing tide in Breton fortunes. This would seem a fitting memorial, binding the location to its historical experience, with subject and landscape combining to quicken the effect.

The **Quiberon peninsula** is intense with memorials, offering many forms of *memento mori*, even leaving aside its density of megaliths, which were after all the earliest form of monument. It's hard to forget the pathos of a little stele now at Le Fozo acknowledging the sacrifice of American mothers who lost sons fighting for France in WWI. Or the modern menhir on the wild west coast above a creek made terrifying by high tides and gale force winds. It records the awful deaths here in 1979 of two members of the rescue services, Michel Pohin, a fireman, and André Robet, a policeman, who gave their lives trying to save a reckless photographer (aged 21) who had been swept off a rock. And who survived. The carving is crude, with a large etched cross dominating the basic words recording this tragically pointless loss of life of heroes trying to save '*un imprudent*'. The power of under-statement. And a potent reminder that there are so many ways of dying and only one death.

This area was also the site of an even more calamitous event at the end of the 18th century, which resulted in the execution of 748 men, 167 of them at Quiberon itself. On the approach to the peninsula, the Chouan museum in a bunker at Plouharnel charts the ill-fated Catholic monarchist movement opposed to the new Republic. In addition to the famous uprising in the Vendée, certain areas of Brittany made their own passionate protests against the Republican 'patriots' and particularly against the persecution of priests who refused to swear an oath of loyalty to the new constitution. These men were forced into hiding, carrying out services in secret and even blessing the guns of the Chouan fighters who tried to protect them.

The Chouans operated in different parts of Brittany in separate groups, each under their own leader, and their methods were those of guerilla warfare rather than the more organised units of the contemporary Vendée war. The Breton rebels grew in stature and daring as they eluded Republican soldiers through intimate knowledge of the countryside and extensive support from the peasant population. Many young men escaped official conscription in their ranks, joining the roving bands who attacked Republican convoys, infrastructure and targeted individuals. Southern Morbihan, including the Quiberon peninsula, was particularly strong in Catholic resistance, under the staunch leadership of Georges Cadoudal.

In June 1795, a group of more than 5000 *emigrés*, nobles and their followers who had left France to escape the Revolution, returned with English backing for their attempt to unite the counter-revolutionary forces of western France against the new government in Paris. They landed at dawn on the 27th on beaches at Carnac, but were soon under pressure from the Republican forces of General Hoche. It proved impossible for the disparate groups and diverse leaders of *emigrés* and Chouans to come together with coherent plans and agreed chains of command. The local population were also embroiled in all the manoeuvrings as the Catholic forces were driven back into the Quiberon peninsula, where they established themselves in the Fort de Penthièvre. English ships lay off the west coast to support them, but their constructive contribution ultimately lay in taking aboard those fleeing from the inevitable debacle as Hoche closed in. The fort was taken thanks to betrayal by ex-Republicans purporting to have joined the opposite cause, and the remaining royalist forces finally surrendered on the shore at Quiberon, believing their lives saved by this ultimate step. Initially promises seem to have been given, but it was not to be. Hoche was soon away fighting elsewhere and revolutionary councils in Paris were making different decisions. Seven hundred and forty-eight men were condemned and summarily executed.

Two contrasting memorials in Quiberon reflect both sides in this terrible confrontation, and the ongoing, bitter split between Whites (Catholic conservatives) and Blues (progressive Republicans) which was to dominate 19th century politics in Brittany. They signal the underlying significance of many such monuments, to put forward one point of view in an effort to ensure the lasting record of partisan action. The **Monument aux Emigrés** is a very basic flat-topped pyramidal stele sitting by the Plage de Porigo near Port Haliguen on the eastern coast of the peninsula. Its message is equally simple: 'Here, on the 27th July 1795, the Emigrés surrendered to General Hoche.' The road beside it is named the Boulevard des Emigrés, indicating local political acknowledgement and a certain honouring of the memory of these unfortunate men, and what they represent: the defence of tradition and the Church, which had begun to reassert itself in Breton life as soon as the Revolution was over.

It was an action by the priest of Quiberon in 1895 that led to the counter-offensive of a huge grandiose tribute to Lazare Hoche himself. This provocation was the proposal to build a chapel to honour the memory of the *emigré* martyrs and house their remains, which provoked a furious reaction from the Republican faction, now in political control of the town. The 'Bleus de Bretagne' started a subscription to raise the necessary money for their own monument, a **statue of General Hoche**, and the state was also ready to contribute to such a cause. They commissioned a bronze statue from sculptor Jules Dalou, a staunch republican himself. It was finally erected in 1902, after some opposition from Hoche's own grandson who condemned their motives. A government minister attended the event which took place in the main square of Quiberon, given a name change to Place Hoche. And there it still stands, despite an early challenge in 1910 when a VIVE LE ROI placard was attached and an attempt to blow it up by the Breton Revolutionary Army, part of the Breton Liberation Front (FLB), in 1972.

The statue was moved from its central spot to a rather unobtrusive corner of the square in 2013, but its impressive size and structure still impose. The bronze statue of Hoche stands on a rocky base, part solid and unyielding, part the rippling contours of a promontory, where he gazes out to sea. It is fairly conventional for a protest monument, but the plaque proudly records the initiative of the 'Blues of Brittany' to get the thing done by raising the necessary funds. Various luminaries of the Republican establishment supported the move, from the League of the Rights of Man to great folklorist Anatole Le Braz, who wrote a poem in honour of Hoche. Destroyer of the strongly supported Chouans Hoche may have been, but he had an extraordinary military career throughout the febrile Revolutionary years. It's quite a shock to take in the dates (1768-1797). He was only 29 when he died of tuberculosis, having just taken up command of the Rhine armies.

The most ubiquitous memorials, in every commune in the land, are commemorations of the two World Wars, often with the statue of a single soldier to represent the tragic losses that so marred village life in the 20th century. Lists of names of the dead show how families suffered over and over again, and hint at consequences long beyond the fate of a single individual. The replication of grief is almost unimaginable to those of us who have not lived through a major war. The town of Quiberon's **WWI memorial** incorporates a menhir, which while not unique in Brittany, was felt to have a particular significance on this peninsula so dense with neolithic remains. The chosen stone is very large (6m high and 2.2m at the base) and has a most imposing presence. It was brought here specially from the nearby hamlet of Manémeur, where two sizeable standing-stones remain upright beside the coast road. Apparently it took a week to transport for the inauguration on 6th November, 1921, and this process cost a noteworthy 2000 francs.

Interestingly, the original documents of deliberations about the monument state clearly that the architects (a firm in Vannes) were instructed 'to carry out a very simple project, avoiding banality, and preserving a fitting character for a region known for its megaliths'. They certainly chose one very arresting stone. The monument at the top of a narrow street leading up from Place Hoche is eloquent. The immense stone itself emanates the sense of undisturbed eternity and absolute solidity, while three towering trees, one with fabulously twisted trunk and spreading canopy, frame the ensemble. The whole is a self-contained statement, embodying the trauma of the past carried through into the future by the power of memory, expressively suitable for its purpose of commemorating those lost in war.

Collective memorials cover a range of situations, but death and loss are their perennial themes. The grief of women waiting at home for beloved menfolk away at sea or fighting in wars, is a subject of many monuments in Brittany, particularly in coastal communities. Sculptor **Réné Quivillic** (1879-1969) from Plouhinec was renowned for his portrayal of such figures in monuments to the victims of war, such as the famous ensemble of womenfolk on the quay at Pont l'Abbé. In his native village, he used his mother as a model for the full-sized granite form of a woman in mourning, incorporated into the war memorial. This emphasis on the parent or partner rather than the lost soldier was typical of his conception. He started out working with wood and later produced some amazing engravings, such as an unforgettable image from 1945 of the outline of Brittany as a dragon's head eating dead sailors, whose bodies float like a shoal of sardines all around the coast. He is best remembered today, however, as the *'imagier de la douleur bretonne'* (the sculptor of Breton grief), a headline used by the paper *La Dépêche* in 1927 with reference to one of his most famous works.

In that year, the headland of the **Pointe Saint-Mathieu** on Brittany's Atlantic coast was chosen out of many places in France for an official monument in tribute to the sailors lost in WWI. Quivillic was the chosen artist. A former guard-house on the cliff-top plateau was used to create a permanent exhibition of remembrance, featuring an eloquent display of photographs of the dead, heart-rending to study, and details of all the ghastly shipwrecks that led to their deaths. Outside, near the edge of the cliff, is the **stele**, 17m high in kersanton stone, topped by the bust of a woman, head to one side and covered, with her gaze towards the ground, hands clasped under her chin in prayer. Or perhaps resignation, as there is no sign of hope in that suffering face. The text below is simple: AUX MARINS 1914-1918. Set into the block

Monument aux marins 1914-1918, Pointe Saint-Mathieu

under that, Quivillic has added a relief carving with the contrastingly callow face of a young seaman. Apart from the names of France's major ports, the only other decoration are square blocks of symbolic representations of marine activity: ships, a submarine, fish, waves, an anchor, a compass rose and a star. There is no religious emblem on this official Republican memorial, despite its Breton context. The impression, allied with those distressing photographs in the cenotaph, is stark, but seems to echo fittingly those abiding Breton motifs of the closeness of life and death, and the eternal rhythms of the sea that have governed the lives of so many men and women for good or ill for so long. As a child, Quivillic himself suffered the loss of a brother at sea.

Sometimes memorials have no heroic element, no wide appeal to patriotism or necessary sacrifice. Sometimes they are just about ordinary people and extraordinary tragedy. Sometimes they have no words at all, but only sadness. That the rocks around **Penmarc'h**, the south-west tip of Brittany, are dangerous has been well known for a very long time. Chaucer's *Franklin's Tale* hangs on the magical 'disappearance' of these obstacles to Dorigen's husband's safe return from England. Many ships have come to grief in their passage along this low prickly coast, but that is hardly surprising, perhaps not even shocking. But one comparatively recent event of quite another kind lingers in the memory here. This one is hard to believe, even as I have often stood in the spot where it occurred, listening to the waves slap and die in the crevices below, watching the deep blue of the sea against the bright leucogranite rocks in their crazy formation, sticking up in a defiant fringe against the elemental powers they face.

Tourists labour up the stones to grasp at the handrail on the most prominent ridge, raking the wide views across to Audierne and Cap Sizun with their cameras and binoculars. The **Rochers de**

Saint-Guénolé stand firm in the face of the endless ocean, their horrible secret enshrined just beyond the railing, where a flat rock below has an iron cross embedded in the surface. This is the most basic of memorials to members of a family who were swept away by a freak wave after enjoying a picnic on a bright day, 10th October 1870. On this low coastline, five people lost their lives and only three bodies were ever found. To this day foolhardy sightseers and photographers play the game of chance with the sea on these rocks in far more dramatic weather conditions than that fateful occasion. Some still lose, but the double allure of the exorbitant stones and the heaving tide prove an eternal temptation. They have no memorials on this perilous shore, other than a notice of general reminder that danger is ever-present here.

The Prefect of Finistère and his family were relaxing one fine day on the rocks above a calm sea. They had picnicked there, and about three o'clock in the afternoon were dispersed in little groups, chatting. Gustave-Léonard Pompon-Levainville and his sister-in-law Madame Dresch were talking with Paul du Chatellier, a well-known painter and archaeologist beside his little cabin at the foot of the rocks. The others were still up at the summit, his wife Marie-Louise with her niece and nephew, and a short distance away, her own daughter Gabrielle and Madame Bonnemain, the governess. In an instant that tranquil family scene was shattered. Out of nowhere a huge wave formed from the depths of the Trou d'Enfer (Hole of Hell) below and mounted the rocks. A child's cry was heard 'An tarzh!' (a breaker), but there was no time to do anything to save them. All five were swept away.

The recovered victims were buried in Benodet, where the Prefect lived until his death in 1894. It was a deeply upsetting tragedy for the local inhabitants, and in the way of popular culture in Brittany, laments were quickly written and distributed at local fairs, referring to the Prefect's or the Victims' Rock. But there was a distasteful sequel. Relatives of Madame Levainville from the Bourdon family wanted to know if she died before her daughter or vice versa, hoping that they, rather than her husband, would inherit her estate. At the court case in Rennes, every minute detail of the calamity was pored over, with witnesses called to establish exactly who had been where, and details of the state of the recovered

bodies examined. And all for nothing in the end, as they lost their claim when the Prefect's wife was deemed to have died first.

The iron cross on the rocks at Saint-Guénole tells no story. It means nothing to those visitors who do not already know of the event. After all, it's not unusual to see that Christian image in Brittany, and this one, small and flat, barely registers as the majestic scene of nature's finest spectacle opens so extensively before anyone who clambers up to the top. Only the timeless stones support the ghosts of that party, and carry the memory of the inconceivable moment when a carefree family outing turned into the drama of death.

Memento mori and all that.

12 Ex-stones

If the stones of Brittany are powerful conduits of human imagination, and compelling in their frequency in the landscape, we should perhaps end by trying to conjure up a little of what has been lost. There always seem to be plenty of neolithic remains to visit, but these probably represent a mere fraction of the original total. This could be the longest chapter in the book, as we know from the work of those who have painstakingly recorded the megaliths that no longer exist, but that is too disappointing a story to dwell on at length. We can only acknowledge that the action of time, weather, landowners, treasure-seekers and other individuals has taken inestimable toll on the lithic treasures that human effort once embedded so liberally in this corner of Europe. Some of the fallen can be listed by name and location with photographic evidence to endure in a shadowy world of theoretical existence, even if searchers on the ground will find only empty space. How unimaginable are the numbers of silent others that have vanished without any trace whatsoever. The web is broken, never to be reformed, but these are special spaces, physically void yet holding the whisper of those lost stones.

It is sobering to think that the huge cairn of **Barnenez** (see p.54) once had a partner nearby. This smaller version (but still 30m in length) to the north-west of the remaining monument was completely destroyed in 1954 at the beginning of hostilities orchestrated by local officials to facilitate the creation of a new road to bring tourists and stimulate the post-war economy. This motivation is ironic considering the later cultural value placed on megalithic remains as a draw for visitors. Only the prompt action of a local journalist, Francis Gourvil, and his urgent appeal to renowned archaeologist Pierre-Roland Giot, who had already surveyed the site, put an end to this wilful destruction and saved the larger cairn for the rarity it is today.

Many individual menhirs in Brittany have been moved for a variety of reasons or simply bitten the dust, being broken for re-use, and the slabs of dolmens and alley graves have been recycled into the paving of many roads, or served to prop up walls and buildings. A register of lost megaliths in Côtes d'Armor (see p.221) includes the following typical entries:

> Dolmen - recorded in 1921 as having lost its capstone, today all gone.
>
> Menhir - 4,8m, moved a distance of 2km in 1965 for 'shamelessly commercial' reasons. Now nothing remains of this monument.
>
> Alignment of 64 small dolerite stones, destroyed for main road between Rennes and Dinan, a few of them used to decorate a rest area on the route.

Bald statements like this catalogue of casualties are a sober reminder that what does remain today, rich though it may be, is but a fragment of the original whole. Even more telling is the loss of monuments actually caught on camera before the event. One example is the **allée couverte du Rocher** once located in the

Allée couverte du Rocher (from an old postcard)

commune of Saint-Jacut-du-Méné. A postcard of 1909 preserves the memory of this dilapidated but substantial ruin, standing 14m in length. It had been excavated in 1897 with modest finds of pottery shards, bones and the touching detail of a 'small holed stone'. The tomb was sold to a stone-mason in 1910 and completely destroyed, and apparently no outcry of any sort greeted that transaction and its consequences.

Natural stones have also suffered at the hands of man, for practical or even, incredibly, moral reasons. During the Occupation, Germans exploited the protective cordon of pebbles, nearly 50m wide, along the **Bay of Audierne**, which offered a natural barrier against the incursions of the sea. It stretches from Penhors almost to the famous Pointe de la Torche, and had been protected in 1934 by a decree to preserve its integrity, so vital to safeguarding the interior. But for the Germans there was an insatiable need for material to build the numerous structures of the Atlantic Wall defence system and other projects around roads and stations. A TODT camp (forced labour for construction projects) had already been set up at Tréguennec in 1942 and the following year a factory (**usine à galet**) right on the coast was added to churn large quantities of the preventative pebbles into concrete. They projected using about a million cubic tons in total. After the war local enterprises continued to exploit the barrier, up to the point where floods burst through in the winter of 1966, but it was not until the 1990s that the problem was seriously addressed and concerted attempts were made to re-fortify the dunes of this exposed coastline. The large eerie remains of the factory's dominant structure can still be seen today, including the great silos and rails laid to transport the resulting materials from shore to Pont l'Abbé. A reminder that destruction works on many levels.

At the other end of the scale, a further example of wilful destruction that might be amusing if it wasn't so brutish is the destruction of the **Zizi de Pipi** (Grandpa's Willy) at Plouescat in 1987. This penis-shaped rock on the beach at Porsmeur attracted the censure of prudes and the celebration of admirers, with someone painting it red every year to highlight the unfortunate form still further, although it would have been hard for anyone to miss the connection. The municipal council made the decision to dynamite the poor rock, innocent victim of human censure. This was one case where celebrity was not welcomed by the powers that be. Soon after, another target of attention was found in a handy nearby rock formation taking the name *Les fesses de mamie* or Grandma's Bottom...

There are some strange halfway houses in the existence of megaliths that are neither fully with us nor completely obliterated. The **Alignement de la Madeleine** in **Penmarc'h** offers a tantalising glimpse of what must be one of the greatest losses, and, from a monument on a scale approaching Carnac, we can loosely trace the dwindling numbers of standing-stones here over about a hundred years. At the south-west tip of Finistère, this megalithic

Alignement de la Madeleine

wonder consisted of four rows of stones, orientated roughly east/west and extending over a kilometre, already diminished from their original form when first properly recorded in 1867 by Armand du Chatellier. He made a plan of the site, calculating from the existing statistics that 600-700 stones must once have made up the alignment. By 1887 many more had disappeared, according to his son, who continued the surveillance. Gabriel Puig de Ritalongi published a book in 1894 recording three lines and including speculation on their purpose, from the general religious and military significance to a more specific funerary function. He also noted a cromlech at the western end and dolmens plus a tumulus to the east, indicating the complexity of the site. A map made in 1920 for a work on the megaliths of Pays Bigouden shows the remaining stones. A few were still there in the mid 20th century, but these completely disappeared during the 1960s.

Local legend to account for their origins says Mary Magdalene threw pebbles down onto the Devil to oust him from the area. This was a clear success, as there is no sign of him in Penmarc'h today and the lady has her chapel still, giving her name to the neolithic alignment (which is also known locally as the *Alignement de Lestriguiou*). The secretly situated, beautiful chapel is on the site of a former leper house, with the surviving indications of a statue of Saint Lazarus (patron of sufferers of the disease) and holes at the base of the main supporting arch that may indicate where a grill was placed to separate the priest from his unfortunate flock. The interior is flooded with a wonderful light these days from the refulgent modern windows (1981) of master craftsman Jean Bazaine.

It is galling to reflect on the probable extent of neolithic remains once standing here at the very edge of Brittany. But in fact all is not utterly lost and the alignment has recently made a sort of ghostly comeback. In the 1990s, after a series of large menhirs were found buried in the dunes, an association saw to their resurrection in tribute to the original neolithic mass construction. They now stand in a well-spaced line along a walking path on the edge of fields, about 300m from the chapel, impressive even in this thin form, memorial to the exceptional monuments that once stood here, in one of the richest areas of megaliths in Brittany.

Plenty of other placed stones in the area suggest that this was indeed once a vast site of repeated prehistoric use and varied purpose over long periods of time, like Carnac. As it is not such a well-known part of Brittany, perhaps it is worth mentioning here that still in fine existence not far away from the alignment site are the two standing-stones of Kerscaven, each placed in proximity to small streams: the Menhir de la Vierge (6m), the widest standing-stone I've ever seen, and the impressive Menhir de l'Eveque (6.5m), which has a singular ridged shape, (almost) resembling the mitre of a bishop, hence the name. (The latter is on private land and only visible from the road.) The Dolmen de Lestriguiou is also nearby, described on an early postcard as a *menhir*, but actually quite substantial remains of an *allée couverte*, despite having a corner chipped off in the interests of modern transport.

A final image can be drawn from **Loctudy**. The mysterious dolmen on (or under) the **Plage d'Ezer** is neither here nor there, coming and going in completely unpredictable fashion. It was discovered on the beach by chance during a Sunday outing in 1950 by eminent scholar Pierre-Roland Giot, who was director of the prehistory museum of Finistère at Pors Carn in Penmarc'h. He observed nine stones in oval shape, roughly aligned north/south. He went on to excavate the site and was able to give an approximate date of 4500BC. The situation was precarious, however, and not all artefacts could be extracted for fear of destabilising the stones which had to withstand those natural forces constantly shaping the coastal environment. Soon after, the dolmen disappeared under the sand with movement of what once had been high dunes on one side and the power of the tides on the other. An aerial survey of 1952 showed no sign of the stones. This tenacious megalith was presumed 'lost' for the next sixty-four years. Then in 2014 the results of a great storm revealed the very top of the rocks before the sand buried them once more. The next appearance was recently, in February 2021, as the result of another tempest, but now all traces have gone again. Perhaps as weather conditions become more and more extreme and water levels rise, it may be lost to us forever, but eternally existent in a submarine realm.

There when not there. Less a phantom, more a survival of stones. I have never seen it but I'm happy to know it endures under the top layer of this changeable world. Let it represent all those countless others subsumed by shadows of one kind or another. *Dalc'homp soñj*! *Souvenons-nous*! Let us remember.

ACKNOWLEDGEMENTS

Firstly, my gratitude to Jack Fraser, who knows both Brittany and its stones well. I discovered these affinities long ago from Twitter #DailyMegalith, and I'm delighted she agreed to write the foreword to this book

Secondly, I would like to thank the following friends for their part in the book's journey:

Nicolas Adell (University of Toulouse), who gave me the inspirational nudge for Stone Stories after we met through his own work, an ethnographical study on the subject
Pierres vivantes (Living stones)

Alan Montgomery, historian of Roman Scotland, great companion for Brittany exploration and super-illustrator, for his wonderful enhancement of my text

Phil Watson and Julia Kirby for their friendship, megalith talk, and an introduction to all the invaluable evidence contained in old postcards of Brittany

Yves Marhic, for his exceptional help with finding things, and his never-failing enthusiasm for correcting my attempts at reference to the Breton language

Vicki Trott, Patricia Stoughton, Suzie Grogan, fellow-writers, who all read sections of the manuscript and gave very helpful feedback

And finally to note that Trevor Thorn did his absolute best to stop me writing anything at all

FURTHER READING

<u>COLLECTIONS OF FOLKLORE</u>

Théodore Hersart de la Villemarqué (1815-1895)
  Le Barzaz Breiz
Anatole Le Braz (1859-1926)
  La Légende de la Mort
  Au pays des pardons
Émile Souvestre (1806-1854)
  Les Derniers Bretons
  Le Foyer breton
Adolphe Oran (1834-1918)
  Trésor des contes du pays gallo
  Chansons de Bretagne
Paul Sébillot (1843-1918)
  Croyances, mythes et légendes des pays de France
  Contes de la Haute Betagne

<u>MODERN WORKS</u>

Phil Watson's masterly collection based on old postcards:
  Vol 1 The Megaliths of Carnac (2018)
  Vol 2 The Megaliths of Morbihan, excluding Carnac (2018)
  Vol 3 The Megaliths of Finistère (2018)
  Vol 4 The Megaliths of Côtes d'Armor and Ille-et-Vilaine (2019)
  Vol 5 The Megaliths of Loire-Atlantique and Vendée (2020)
Pierre-Roland Giot
  La Bretagne des mégalithes (Ouest-France, 2007)
Bernard Rio
  Voyage dans l'au-delà, les Bretons et la mort (Ouest-France, 2013)
Christophe Auray
  Pierres magiques et guérisseuses de Bretagne (Ouest-France, 2018)
Barry Cunliffe
  Bretons and Britons: The Fight for Identity (OUP, Oxford, 2021)
Wendy Mewes
  Brittany: a cultural history (Signal Books, 2014)

<u>USEFUL WEBSITES</u>

  megalithes-breton.fr (wide ranging site, including registry of lost stones)
  menhirs-carnac.fr
  patrimoine.bretagne.bzh

INDEX of sites and stones
(Italics denote illustrations)

Alignement de la Madeleine 216-217, *216*
Abbaye de Boquen 135, 141
Abbaye de Beauport 172
Abbaye Saint-Mathieu 85
Aber Ildut 69
Aber Wrac'h 107
An Eured Vein (Stone Wedding Party) 37, 172
Armorica 6, 37, 40, 75, 106
Arthur's Grotto 28, 49-50, *51*

Babouin and Babouine .158-160, *159*
Baie d'Audierne 171, 215
Bains-sur-Oust 197, 198
Barnenez 54-56, 213
Baud 115
Bieuzy 66, 116
Brélévenez 39
Brennilis 17, 57, 59
Brest 71, 72, 155, 170, 176
Brignogan Plage 163
'Brocéliande' 52, 53, 101
Buttes de Monthault 186

Camaret 151, 153, 154, 155
Carhaix 38, 40, 41, 149
Carfantin .126
Carnac . . . . .12, 35, 38, 118-123, ... 127, 159, 160, 172, 205, 216
Carnoët 131
Castennec 67, 116
Caurel 166
Cemetery of the 7777 saints . .174-176
Chaos de Mardoul 12, *16*, 17
Chaos du Gouët 32-34
Chapelle Notre-Dame du Kreisker 79-82
Chapelle de Saint-Gildas 66
Chapelle Saint Gonéry 78
Chapelle Saint-Maurice 8
Chapelle de Saint Meldéoc 190

Chapelle Kermaria an Iskuit 196
Château de Coat-an-Noz 134
Château du Guildo . . . . .135-143, ...*136*, 178
Château de Trécesson 44
Coët Correc, allée couverte 166-169, *168*
Colonne des Trente 198, 201
Combourg 53, 99-100
Commana 60, 77
Corong, Gorges du 29-32, *30*
Côte de Granit rose 19-24, *22*, 44, 118, 132
Créhen 178

Daoulas .4, 44
Dirinon 188, 189
Dol-de-Bretagne . . . . .53, 95, ... 100, 124, 126, 127
Dolmen de Lestriguiou 218
Douarnenez 2, 91, 97

Église de Lambour 147-151
Église Saint-Nonne 189
Elven 143, 146
Erdeven 123
Er Lannec .96
Essé 127

Fontaine de Barenton .102-104, *102*
Fontaine de Margatte 100
Fontaine de Saint Gildas 111
Forêt du Cranou 1, 2
Forêt de Paimpont . . . . .35, 52, ...53, 59, 101
Forêt de Quénécan 161
Forteresse de Largoët .143-147, *145*

Gavrinis 157, 158
Goulven .110
Grand Rocher 108
Guern 190

Guimiliau 77, 82
Guingamp 10
Guirnivit, allée couverte 96
Guisseny 93

Huelgoat 18, 24-29, 39,
. . . . .44, 49, 50, 52, 118, 181
Hermitage of Saint Hervé . . .63-4, *64*

Île de Batz 65, 106
Île de Bréhat 172-3
Île Carn .38
Île de Groix 91
Île d'Ouessant 5, 93, 106, 164
Île de Saint Cado 112
Île de Sein 7, 86

Josselin 198, 199, 200

Kerguntuil, allée couverte 61
Kerguntuil, dolmen 59
Kerscaven, menhirs 218

La Bataille 198
La Clarté 20, 23
La Lande de la Rencontre 202
La pierre du diable 187
La pierre aux moines 187
La pierre au sacrifice 187
La Roche Longue 33
La Roche Maurice 196
Lampaul-Guimiliau 77, *78*
Landéan 10
Landerneau 94
Landes du Cragou 37
Landes de Locarn 29
Langon 172
Lannédern 194, *195*
Lannion 39, 164
Lanrivoaré 63, 65, 173
Le Faou .3
Le Mengleuz 37
Le Quillio 53
Le Relec 42
Le Runy 158
Les Causeurs, menhirs 7

Lit de Saint Cado 112
Locmariaquer 157
Locmeltro 190
Locquirec 44
Loctudy 218
Logonna-Daoulas 44
Loqueffret 17
Luzec 46, 48

Magoar 111
Mané Guen 35, 39, 191
Manoir de Coecilian . . .151-155, *152*
Mein zao 39
Mell beniguet 190-192
Mémorial de l'Abolition d'Esclavage .
. 196-197
Men Dogan 181, 183-186
Mené Bré 39-42, *43*
Menec 35, 172
Menez Hom 2, 5, 39
Menez Bel Air 39-40
Menhir du Champ Dolent . . . .
. . . . .118, 124-127, *125*
Menhir des Droits de l'Homme . . . .
. 169-171
Menhir de l'Eveque 218
Menhir de l'Hopital 33
Menhir de Kerampeulven 39
Menhirs de Kergadiou 74-5
Menhir de Kerhouezel 75
Menhir de Kerloas . . .69-72, *70*, 118
Menhir des Landes de Guellec . . .31
Menhir de Prétoquis 33
Menhir de Quelenec 31
Menhir de Saint Uzec . .164-166, *165*
Menhir de la Vierge 218
Menhirs de Lespurit-Quelen 97
Men Marz . . . . . . .163-4, *front cover*
Merlin's tomb 52-54
Mi-voie 198, 199, 201
Monts d'Arrée 10, 17, 25, 37-38,
. . . .42, 44, 45, 59, 77, 172, 177, 195
Mont Dol 40, 42, 53-4, 124
Mont Saint Michel 40, 42, 142
Mont-Saint-Michel-de-Brasparts
 (Menez Mikael) 37, 39, 172

223

Montagnes Noires 35
Monthault 43, 186-188
Monument aux Bretons 202
Monument aux Emigrés 206
Mougau Bihan 38, 60

Nantes 196

Penmarc'h 45, 91, 123,
..................210, 216, 218
Perros-Guirec 19, 21, 24, 105
Petit Menec 25, *36*, 119
Phare de Tévennec 86-88
Pierres sonnantes 178-180, *179*
Pink Granite Coast ....
..........19-24, *22*, 44, 118, 132
Plage de Canté 171
Pleumeur-Bodou 8, *9*, 11, 164
Pleslin-Trigavou 10
Plestin-les-Grèves 107
Ploërmel 198, 199
Plouescat 96, 216
Plouezoc'h 54
Plougastel-Daoulas 45
Plougrescant 78
Plouneour-Menez 77
Plouha 196
Plouharnel 204
Ploumanac'h 20, 24
Plouneour-Lanvern 94
Plounévez-Quintin 53
Plouyé 25, 110
Plussulien 56
Pont l'Abbé 147, 149, 208
Pont Krac'h 107
Pointe du Millier 92
Pointe Saint-Mathieu 208, *209*
Pontsuval 93, 164
Porspoder 94
Prad Paol *106*, 107
Presqu'il de Rhys 121
Primelin 112

Quiberon 203-207
Quimper 2, 25, 81,
.................98, 131, 158, 185

Roc'h Kleger 37
Roc'h Ruz 37
Roc'h Toul 38, 46-49
Roc'h Trévézel 37
Roche aboyante 173
Roche écrianté 187
Roche aux Fées ...118, 127-131, *128*
Roche Tremblante 181-183, *182*
Rochers de Saint Guénolé ..211-212
Rumengol 1-5, 99

Saint-Aubin-du-Cormier 133,
.....................*133*, 202
Saint Conogan's stone boat ...92, *92*
Saint Guyomard 8
Saint Herbot 17, 18
Saint-Just 118
Saint-Malo 147
Saint-Pol-de-Léon 65, 79, 106
Saint-Quay-Portrieux 105
Saint-Thégonnec 45
Saint Tugen 111
Sainte-Tréphine 160, *162*

Tables des Marchands 157
Ti-ar-Boudiged (dolmen) 57, *58*
Toul ar Laerien 38
Trédion 158
Trédrez 35
Trégastel 59, 61, 83
Trégastel, calvaire 83-84, *83*
Tréguennec 215
Trégunc 181, 183
Tressé, allée couverte 61-63

Vallée des Saints 131
Vallée des Traouiero 20
Venus de Quinipily ..67, 113-117, *114*

WWI Memorial,
    Pointe Saint-Mathieu 208, *209*
WWI Memorial, Quiberon 207

Ys 2, 97-9